Date Due

DEC 17 1970		
MAR 24 1971		
OCT 28 1971		
JUN 16 1972		
DEC 30 1978		
FEB 20 1981		
FEB 15 1996		
MAR 20 1997		

DEMCO NO. 38-298

THE NEW CITY

the new city

NATIONAL COMMITTEE ON URBAN GROWTH POLICY

ALBERT RAINS, chairman, LAURANCE HENDERSON, director

THE NATIONAL ASSOCIATION OF COUNTIES

THE NATIONAL LEAGUE OF CITIES

THE UNITED STATES CONFERENCE OF MAYORS

URBAN AMERICA INC.

Edited by **DONALD CANTY**

Published for URBAN AMERICA INC. by

FREDERICK A. PRAEGER, Publishers

NEW YORK • WASHINGTON • LONDON

Frederick A. Praeger, Inc., Publishers

111 Fourth Avenue, New York, N.Y. 10003, U.S.A.

5, Cromwell Place, London S.W. 7, England

Published in the United States of America in 1969
by Frederick A. Praeger, Inc., Publishers

Library of Congress Catalog Card Number: 69–83782

Design — Production by Hubert W. Leckie / Susan Lehmann

Manufactured in the United States of America by
Double Dot Press, Inc., Washington, D. C.

FOREWORD

Spiro T. Agnew
Vice President of the United States of America

to those responsible for urban planning and administration, the problems faced by American cities seem an unending chain of crises. Not only are suggested solutions few, but the general ability to think through the intricate maze of political, technical and geographic interrelationships is almost totally lacking. Often the most expert in one problem area find it impossible to compensate for difficulties totally alien to their field of expertise.

More evident every day is the unalterable fact that the problems of a contemporary city do not end at the city boundaries; that adjacent urban areas, usually part of a county, are suffering from an extension of the same crises. Therefore, the problems must be attacked by all levels of government and all portions of the private sector. They are of such magnitude that they can only be conquered by a concerted effort, and the most serious error that we make is to continue to think of them simply as "the problems of the cities."

Apparent to every individual who encounters a modern metropolitan area are the culprits—traffic congestion, pollution, blight and overcrowding. The structural problems are easy to locate and diagnose. The problems which register upon the senses can be found with little effort. Most of these are soluble by expenditures of money and the provision of technical capability. Even the problem of environmental sanitation is discoverable far in advance of its attaining critical proportion.

But nearly invisible, yet most urgent, are the purely human and social aspects of urban decline. Human costs cannot be computed in dollars, for human life and human dignity are not commodities. A society which treats them as such does so at its peril.

Everyone concerned knows that something must be done. Without cities of a new kind, cities which exist to serve human life and not detract from it, our complex civilization cannot survive. This book speaks of several ways of creating these new cities: by making new the old, by expanding small towns, by organizing peripheral growth so that it produces planned communities instead of sprawl—and by building them from the ground up, either as satellites to existing cities or as entirely new urban centers far removed from the old. I would like particularly to address myself to these last two approaches.

The concept of satellite cities, while not new, has been tried in this country to a limited extent, largely during the past decade. A satellite city is not just another suburb, or bedroom town. It is a self-sustaining economic entity, a truly new city where people work, shop, play and sleep. It is planned for optimum living conditions, optimum, not maximum, land use, and an economic and social spectrum of inhabitants and activities. Its industries, and its sources of income, are diversified. It has a satellite relationship to an older city, not only in terms of geography, but also in terms of the kinds of regional identities which exist among cities with common interests. The planning of these new cities offers opportunities to preserve the natural environment, and often to improve the surrounding countryside. Planned satellites offer a chance to develop new transportation systems, new housing and merchandising patterns, and orderly control of vehicles, giving human beings priority over machines.

Satellite cities must be considered within their natural limitations, foremost among which is that they are, as their name suggests, ancillary to a primary urban center. They must depend upon a central city for the unique services which it can supply to them in common. The satellite must have a balance of residential, commercial and industrial uses, but it need not provide such services as an airport, a stadium, a civic center, a port or art museums. These are facilities designed to serve a larger segment of the population, and the presence of an efficient transportation system makes them available to residents of several satellites. It is obvious that use frequencies for these facilities are generally not on a daily basis, so it is reasonable to expect that they not be as proximate to residential areas as a place of work or a store.

The step beyond the satellite city is the completely new city, placed in a location which offers its planners maximum opportunity for engagement with the future. This concept was boldly originated in America in the 18th century, and two cities, both of which still exist, were then planned by the same man for two different purposes. Pierre L'Enfant laid out the plans for what is now Paterson, New Jersey, as the Federal Manufactory, before he began work on Washington, D. C., as the seat of the Federal Government. His plans for Paterson were realistically centered on maximum utilization of the waterpower technology of the period, but they were never executed because of lack of funds. Even in Washington, his visions and expectations were so far ahead of the technology of his time that it was nearly a century before the city he planned began to emerge from woods, fields and swamps.

Since then, other countries have experimented with new cities, generally to provide a seat for government. Yet today, as at no time in the past, the concept of the new city is technically feasible in terms of power, transportation, communication and the preservation and use of natural resources.

Transmission of electricity and natural gas makes it possible for us to be at any distance from a source of power; rail, highway and air make the rapid movement of people and commodities merely a choice of the extent to which each means is to be utilized; our communications facilities are so highly developed that they threaten to swamp us with information no matter where we may be located. We have the technology and knowledge available to enable us to use whatever natural resources we have without ruining them. It only remains for us to put into practice what we possess as theory. However, in planning, we must remember to keep our options open: Our technology, even our sources of power, can change so rapidly in the near future that much of what we consider today may become as obsolete as the water-driven factories which L'Enfant planned for.

Planning for completely new cities allows us to consider the rational distribution of industry on a national scale. Perhaps we will have to change some of the relationships of our economy to strengthen it, to provide humane and useful futures for those people who now seem to have none, to offer more dramatic challenges to our young people, and to give a sense of being needed and useful to the increasing numbers of our older citizens.

The concept of the new city offers us a chance to discover what we really want from an urban environment, and what we plan to bring to it. Unlike planning for a single aspect of urban life, the planning for the new city involves fresh examination of nearly every concept we have taken for granted. It promises an intellectual understanding as great as that of the space age itself.

Yet all of these considerations do not preclude the need to continue our efforts to improve the quality of life in our existing cities, and to control urban sprawl. The constant growth of our population confronts us with a desperate race against time if we are to preserve our environment and keep our culture from disintegrating. The year 2000 and a predictable population of more than 300 million are closer than we care to think.

THE NEW CITY explores these matters in dimensions of the past, present and future. It offers a challenge to our ways of thinking about urban problems, and our methods of action and reaction. It deserves the attention of everyone concerned with the problems of urban survival. For whether or not one agrees with the views it presents, THE NEW CITY offers the kind of stimulation which is germane to any serious thought of our future environment, and that is a large achievement for any book.

THE AUTHORS

HENRY BAIN is a senior associate at the Washington Center for Metropolitan Studies. He participated in the preparation of the Year 2000 Plan for the National Capital Region, the Washington Regional Open-Space Project, the 1985 Comprehensive Plan for the District of Columbia, and the planning for the new town of Columbia. He is the author of a monograph entitled "The Development District: A Governmental Institution for the Better Organization of the Urban Development Process in the Bi-County Region," prepared for the Maryland-National Capital Park and Planning Commission.

CARL FEISS, FAIA, AIP, is a planning and urban design consultant and frequently lectures on architecture and city planning. He was a special consultant to the National Commission on Urban Problems and to the White House Conference on Natural Beauty. He is a contributor to *Architectural Forum, Progressive Architecture, Architectural Record,* and *Law and Contemporary Problems.* He serves on the board of trustees of the National Trust for Historic Preservation.

HAROLD C. FLEMING, president of the Potomac Institute, was formerly executive director of the Southern Regional Council. He was a special consultant to the White House Conference "To Fulfill These Rights." He is the co-author of "Integration North and South" and has been a contributor to the *New York Times Magazine, The New Republic, Daedalus,* and *City Magazine.*

WILLIAM C. FINLEY is vice president of community development for the Rouse Company. In 1967 he was cited by *Engineering-News Record* magazine for an outstanding contribution to the construction industry in the planning of the new city of Columbia. He was formerly director of the National Planning Commission and vice chairman of the National Capital Housing Authority.

PETER PAUL is a partner of Associated Architects and Planners, Baltimore. While serving as assistant director of the Policy Center of Urban America Inc., he prepared a special study of urbanization of selected metropolitan areas.

WILLIAM L. SLAYTON, executive vice president of Urban America Inc., served for five years as commissioner of the U.S. Urban Renewal Administration. He was also redevelopment director of the National Association of Housing and Redevelopment Officials and vice president for planning and redevelopment for Webb and Knapp Inc., a major U.S. redevelopment firm. He has written extensively in the field of urban renewal and has been awarded the Gold Medal Medallion of the Royal Institution of Chartered Surveyors of Cambridge University, England.

WYNDHAM THOMAS is general manager of the Peterborough Development Corporation of Great Britain and was formerly local chairman of the British new town of Hemel Hempstead. He was a director of Town and Country Planning Association. He is a member of the Land Commission and a board member of the Commission for the New towns.

CONTENTS

11

PREFACE

Albert Rains, Chairman and Laurance Henderson, Director

Since World War II, the housing and urban development policies of the United States have usually been in response to urgent, immediate problems. Confronted by the rapidity of urban growth and change, we have been occupied by coping with events of the present, and have largely neglected the study of broad goals for the pattern of the nation's full growth.

In the drive of our complex efforts to eliminate urban blight and produce some measure of adequate housing, we have paid too little attention to definition of the quality of urban life we are seeking. Without workable concepts of quality—the human and essentially humane basis of city life—the quantitative approach can become statistically satisfying without bettering the conditions we seek to cure. Our failure of vision in this area has already compounded the problems we now face.

For years, the concept of building new cities has been discussed as one of several alternatives to our present policies of haphazard growth around our cities and piecemeal rebuilding or renewal in their cores. New cities would not provide an immediate solution to our urban ills: a minimum lead time of 10 years would be needed for them to become a working reality. In haste for visible results, they have not received consideration as a possible major national program.

To give the new cities concept and other alternatives thoughtful study, the National Committee on Urban Growth Policy was formed in 1968. It is jointly sponsored by the National Association of Counties, the National League of Cities, the United States Conference of Mayors, and Urban America Inc. The members of the Committee represent leaders of all levels of government and both major political parties.

In the fall of 1968, the Committee made an extensive study of European

13

experience in developing new cities over the past 45 years. Meeting at length with the executives of new communities in Great Britain, Sweden, Finland, and Denmark, the Committee members had an excellent opportunity to study the manifold aspects of new city organization. The Committee members followed the development of typical projects from the stage of preliminary planning through completion and economic viability. The trip provided a necessary background for evaluating a potential new cities program in the United States against the operating programs in Europe.

During the early months of 1969, the Committee held a fruitful series of conferences. Under a Ford Foundation grant to Urban America Inc., a broad range of urban experts met with the Committee during these conferences and, in some cases, submitted background papers for its deliberations. A selection of these papers comprises the body of this book, and the Committee's report is its final chapter.

For attending these conferences, and giving their most helpful views, the following have the gratitude of the Committee:

DONALD E. NICOLL, Administrative Assistant to Senator Edmund Muskie

KENNETH MCLEAN, Staff Member, Senate Banking and Currency Committee

WYNDHAM THOMAS, Peterborough Development Corporation, England

STEPHEN PARADISE, Staff Member, Senate Banking and Currency Committee

ALEXIS PALAU, Legislative Assistant to Congressman Jorge Cordova

DR. ANTHONY DOWNS, Senior Vice President, Real Estate Research Corporation, Chicago

WILLIAM G. COLMAN, Executive Director, Advisory Commission on Intergovernmental Relations

CARL FEISS, FAIA, AIP, Planning and Urban Design Consultant

NATHANIEL KEITH, President, National Housing Conference

HAROLD FLEMING, President, Potomac Institute

HONORABLE SAMUEL JACKSON, Assistant Secretary, Department of Housing and Urban Development

HONORABLE JORGE CORDOVA, Congressman, San Juan, Puerto Rico

ROBERT MCCABE, General Manager, New York State Urban Development Corporation

THOMAS WISE, Staff Member, Senate Banking and Currency Committee

CARL HOLMAN, Vice President, Urban Coalition

JAMES GIBSON, Staff Assistant, Potomac Institute

C. MCKIM NORTON, President, Regional Plan Association

PAUL SITTON, Department of Transportation

NATHANIEL ROGG, Executive Vice President, National Association of Home Builders

RICHARD CANAVAN, Staff Vice President, Builders Services Division, National Association of Home Builders

WILLIAM FINLEY, Vice President of Community Development, The Rouse Co.

F. EDWARD CAVIN, Senior Vice President, H. G. Smithy Co.

JOSEPH BARR, Secretary, Department of Community Affairs, Commonwealth of Pennsylvania

JOHN FEILD, Director of Community Relations Service, U. S. Conference of Mayors

HOWARD MOSKOF, Vice President and Treasurer, National Corporation for Housing Partnerships

JOHN ZUCCOTTI, National Corporation for Housing Partnerships

H. CARL MCCALL, former Deputy Administrator, Human Resources Administration, New York City

HONORABLE TERRY SANFORD, President, Urban America Inc.

HUGH FLAHERTY, Secretary, Public Affairs and Legislation, Commonwealth of Pennsylvania

HENRY BAIN, Senior Associate, Washington Center for Metropolitan Studies

JACK JORDAN, Office of the Governor, Commonwealth of Pennsylvania

RICHARD G. LAM, Chairman, Task Force on New Towns, Department of Transportation

JAMES P. TWOMEY, Director, Nonprofit Housing Center, Urban America Inc.

RALPH SCHWARZ, Urban Design and Development Corporation, American Institute of Architects

NATIONAL COMMITTEE ON URBAN GROWTH POLICY

COMMITTEE MEMBERS

ALBERT RAINS, *Chairman*

HALE BOGGS
United States Representative from Louisiana

WILLIAM B. WIDNALL
United States Representative from New Jersey

THOMAS LUDLOW ASHLEY
United States Representative from Ohio

ALBERT W. JOHNSON
United States Representative from Pennsylvania

HENRY S. REUSS
United States Representative from Wisconsin

ROBERT G. STEPHENS, JR.
United States Representative from Georgia

HENRY MAIER
Mayor of Milwaukee, Wisconsin

JOHN SPARKMAN
United States Senator from Alabama

RAYMOND SHAFER
Governor of the Commonwealth of Pennsylvania

PHILIP HOFF
former Governor of the State of Vermont

FLOYD HYDE
Assistant Secretary, Department of Housing and Urban Development and former Mayor of Fresno, California

JAMES ALDREDGE
Commissioner, Fulton County, Georgia

LAURANCE G. HENDERSON,
Director

FRANK DESTEFANO
Assistant Director

JOHN G. TOWER
United States Senator from Texas

CONSULTANTS

JOHN GUNTHER
Executive Director, United States Conference of Mayors

PATRICK HEALY
Executive Director, National League of Cities

BERNARD F. HILLENBRAND
Executive Director, National Association of Counties

WILLIAM L. SLAYTON
Executive Director, Urban America, Inc.

CASEY IRELAND
Minority Staff Member, Housing Subcommittee House Banking and Currency Committee

HAMILTON RICHARDSON
Investment Banker, Dallas, Texas

HUGH MIELDS
Urban Affairs Consultant

JOHN GARVEY JR.
Deputy Executive Director, National League of Cities.

GILLIS LONG
Lawyer and Investment Banker, Alexandria, Louisiana

CARL A. S. COAN
Staff Director, Housing Subcommittee, Senate Banking and Currency Committee

Project director for Urban America's supportive role to the Committee was JONATHAN B. HOWES, director of the Urban Policy Center. Editor of THE NEW CITY, also funded by the Ford Foundation grant, was DONALD CANTY, director of the Urban Information Center. Editorial and photographic research was by LOIS CRAIG, GAIL MILLER, and JAMIE ROSENTHAL of the Information Center staff.

THE CROWDED FUTURE

few words have less graspable meaning than million. Whatever the subject—people, dollars, miles—a million is simply too many of them to mentally picture. When we are told, then, that there are now more than 200 million Americans, that by the end of the century there may well be 300 million, that the additional 100 million added in the coming 30-plus years will live in the urbanized parts of the country, it all sounds abstract.

Its impact, however, will be very real. For the two-thirds of all Americans who now live in metropolitan areas—by Census Bureau definition, cities of at least 50,000 population and their suburbs—these three decades of growth will mean they will be living among nearly twice as many people. Lines will be longer, roads more congested, land harder to find, and everything—beaches, parking lots, buses—will be more crowded. For the other one-third, living in smaller communities outside of the metropolitan rings, the meaning will be quite different: Growth will increase the economic activity of the largest urban areas and will further drain it from the towns and countryside. People who prefer smaller places, a quieter pace, may be forced to choose between their chosen way of life and the chance to make a decent livelihood.

Once America could control its growth by opening and closing the gates of immigration. Now most of our growth is "natural increase"—birth rates which, because people live longer, increasingly exceed death rates. The pace of growth is controlled not by national policy but by millions of individual decisions. Thus growth will be the major fact of American life in the last third of the 20th century whether we, as a nation, like it or not. And with growth, inevitably, will come change.

But the shape of growth can be influenced by national policy. We can, as a nation, decide what kind of change we want it to bring. The decision requires, as a starting point, a look at the patterns of growth in the present and recent past—and what these patterns will produce, if left unchanged, in the crowded future.

THE MEANING OF METROPOLIS

American has built, in this century, a new kind of city. It bears little resemblance to the traditional European cities, which developed as the concentrated and self-contained centers of economic and political life. Instead, its lines of commerce and communication extend to the verdant fringes of metropolitan areas—of metropolis. This new city, metropolis, has many centers rather than one, even though one may predominate. The major center, the urban core, and its diverse suburbs are thoroughly interdependent.

American cities grew up that way, joined to, rather than walled from, the surrounding towns and countryside. Most of what we call urban growth in the 20th century, in fact, has occurred outside of the core. Between 1900 (when eight of ten Americans lived in rural areas) and 1940, the period in which metropolis was born, 40 per cent of all population growth in the country occurred in the suburbs. In the 1940's, half the increase was in the suburbs; in the 1950's, two-thirds. By the mid-1960's, in the aggregate, the core cities had stopped growing altogether.

The outer edges of metropolis were expanding, meanwhile, as new areas were developed and populated. In 1900, the New York metropolitan area covered 752 square miles of land; by 1960, it had spread over nearly 2,000 square miles—and was still spreading. (The Los Angeles metropolitan area was roughly twice as large.) The edges of metropolitan areas were overlapping to form "megalopolis," an unlovely term coined by the French geographer Jean Gottman to describe the continuous urbanized strip running down the Atlantic seaboard from Boston to Washington, D.C.

To complete the portrait of outward expansion, the growth of commerce and industry also shifted to the suburban rings of metropolis. Suburban shopping centers proliferated, themselves grew larger, nearly always containing the kind of major department store that had been part of the definition of "downtown"; factories, whose tall smoke-stacks had ringed the core cities, flattened with the horizontal space demands of automated production and spread over the suburban landscape. From 1954 to 1965, according to the Bureau of Labor Statistics, 63 per cent of all new industrial buildings in metropolis were constructed outside of the core. At present, the bureau's Dorothy K. Newman estimates, 75 to 80 per cent of the new jobs in trade and industry are being created in the metropolitan fringe.

Three factors contributed heavily to the design of metropolis: prosperity, automobility—and public policy. Prosperity meant that millions once consigned to tenements or factory towns could follow their preferences (and in some cases, their work places) to the greenery and detached dwellings of suburbia. The private car freed them from the rigidity and growing inadequacy of public transport, and allowed them to trace new journey-to-work patterns that did not parallel the old rail lines to the core: By 1960, only 16 per cent of the workers in metropolis living in the suburbs had the core as their destination (and 9 per cent of the workers living in the city commuted outward from it.) Public policy, in postwar years, actively cooperated with these trends. Federal and state highway money spread automobility. Federal mortgage guarantees made it easier to buy that detached house and plot of lawn.

It is, however, an overstatement to say that metropolis was consciously designed. It was shaped mainly by the workings of the marketplace responding to the perceived needs, wants, and, as we shall see, fears of millions of American families. The marketplace determined where development would take place and what choices of environment would be offered these striving and mobile households. Public investments in roads, in water and sewer lines, in schools and other facilities followed rather than led the direction of private development, which was, inevitably, ever farther outward where the land was. Public control over the location of development and the quality of environment in metropolis was weak, inadequate to the pressure of urbanization and growth that built up after the war. Metropolis as we know it—this new kind of spread-out city in which nearly 70 per cent of all Americans now live—largely shaped itself.

THE QUALITY OF METROPOLITAN LIFE

Just after the war, a popular theme of books and magazines was that cracks were appearing in the suburban picture window. The writers described the awful homogeneity, the boredom, the sameness of the suburban situation; the destructive impact of increasingly long commutes on family life; the special kinds of delinquency and psychoses bred by it all; the blight of pavement and ticky-tacky houses ("slums of tomorrow") upon the landscape.

Recently there has arisen, in opposition, what might be called the cult of Los Angeles. Taking the American super-city whose citizens are spread most thinly across the semi-tropical terrain, the members of this cult find life there not at all unpleasant. The fact that employment, shopping, and communal facilities (including branches of city hall) are thoroughly decentralized, they say, means more rather than less convenience. The fact that Los Angeles residents are dependent upon the automobile means that they have been able to exercise a preference for independence of movement that most of us share. The reported incidence of mental illness in Los Angeles, they point out, is a fraction of that which researchers have found in Manhattan, at the other end of the density scale. Then the clincher: If Los Angeles is such a bad place, why do droves of people keep coming there?

The truth about the self-shaped pattern of metropolis may be somewhere in between. There is little evidence, to begin with, that the residents of suburbia are painfully dis-satisfied with their environment: The results of what research has been done is to the contrary. The Levittowns of postwar years have not become slums. Instead, their streets now are shaded with trees and their houses have sprouted all manner of modifications and additions over the years that are a tribute to man's determined quest for individu-ality. They are nicer places now than 20 years ago.

In broader terms, it is probably true—although unmeas-ured—that the decentralization of commerce and indus-try has brought workers closer to their jobs, in time if not distance, than in the early urban days of commutation to the core. It is certainly true that the shape of metropolis has helped make homeowners of two-thirds of all Ameri-cans, which is genuine progress. Daniel J. Elazar, a politi-cal scientist at Temple University, has claimed for metropo-lis an even more historic achievement: Its residents enjoy the economic and communications benefits of being ur-banized without being citified in their style of life. In Ela-zar's view, while some Americans like the stimulus of liv-ing in the big city, most do not.

Yet balanced against these claimed advantages are a set of serious, even dangerous, flaws in the metropolitan pat-tern. They afflict the nation's 230-odd metropolitan areas to varying degrees and have only recently begun to rise in the national consciousness. They are, as we shall see, sure

to get worse, not better, with future growth unless cor-rected. In inverse order of significance, they can be sum-marized as follows:

1. The American metropolis is monumentally ugly. Many development houses **are** ticky-tacky; many freeways **do** despoil the landscape (they don't have to, as the parkways around some eastern cities have shown.) The visual en-vironment remains the nation's great cultural blind spot. We are content to look upon wires instead of sky, billboards instead of mountains. The point need not be belabored. It is all around us. It is the visible evidence of the careless-ness, the lack of purpose, we have shown in letting me-tropolis simply grow.

2. A great deal has been left behind in the outward spread of metropolis. The core city historically has been the gen-erator of civilization, of excellence. Out of its intensity of experience, its diversity of population, its richness of cul-tural and intellectual offerings, have come the major indi-vidual and social achievements of this nation as well as others. Many places which the Census calls suburbs are coming to have decidedly urban characteristics; there are now 70 which themselves have populations of 50,000 or more, and some are anything but homogeneous. Neverthe-less, they cannot provide the breadth of experiences, the excitement, the intensity of the core. It has yet to be shown that the **spirit** of the great city can be decentralized.

3. The process of spontaneous urbanization by which me-tropolis has been formed is both wasteful and destructive of natural resources. The most precious of them—land—has been treated not as a resource at all, but as a commodity to be bought, sold, and speculated upon just like any other. Land prices have risen sharply with the spread of metropo-lis—and land speculation has become a major industry.

Urban land, the National Commission on Urban Prob-lems pointed out, is largely a manufactured resource: Its value depends in great part on roads, on water and sewer lines, on a whole "infrastructure" of public services and facilities that make development possible. So far the pub-lic has paid for the infrastructure and the speculator has taken the profits. The difference between open and develop-able land goes into his pocket.

Urbanization is inexorably taking arable land out of production, a fact that the nation, with its almost overly efficient agricultural machine, has not worried much about. But the rate of loss—in California's Santa Clara Valley alone, an average of 3,000 marvelously rich acres per month built over—may someday be a cause of serious regret.

THE PROCESS OF URBANIZATION *begins with the land. It is the basic resource.*

utting on it the collections of buildings and people that are cities, seeing those cities spread.

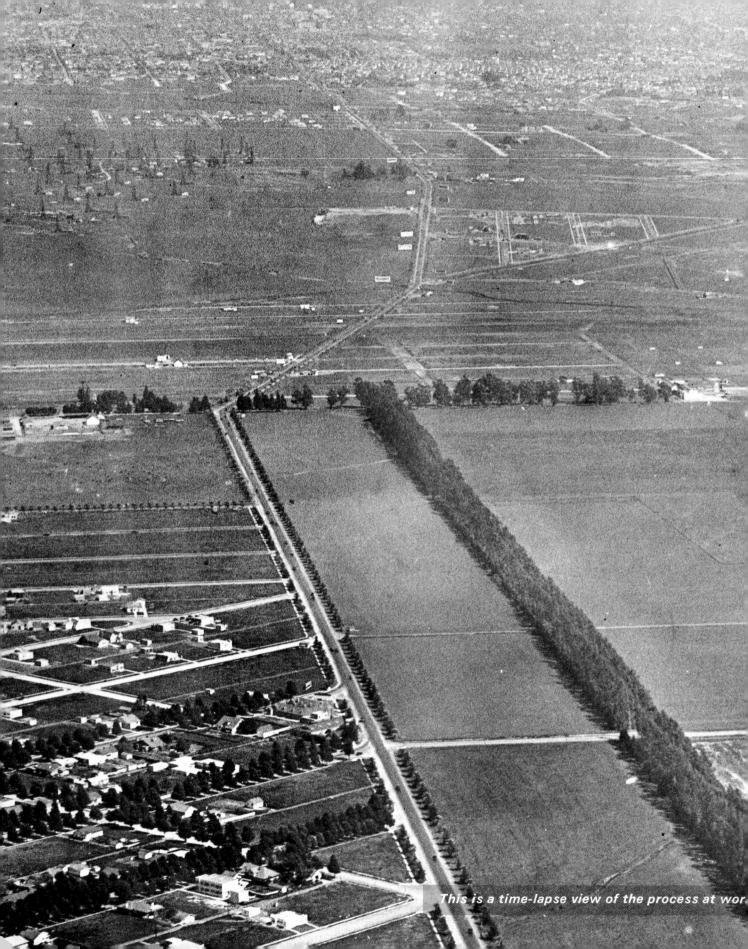

This is a time-lapse view of the process at wor

Wilshire Boulevard, the 16-mile main street of Los Angeles, the 1920's and the 1960's.

This can be the end result of the process. Los Angeles has the lowest density of any major city in America, wi

...say it uses the most land to accommodate the least people over the widest area.

ven around more compact cities, metropolis is growing in the manner of land-eating Los Angeles. As it does, everyth

stretched out, everything is farther apart. This is the land before and after it became Levittown, Pennsylvania.

And so metropolis stretches to the horizon, outward from the core, coagulating into something called mega-lopolis. New York, the nation's image of metropolis, makes fascinating patterns from 35,000 feet in the air. On the ground it doesn't work.

The related scandals of air and water pollution no longer need documentation. They are part of the daily life experiences of millions of metropolitan residents, and something, finally, is being done about them. But it will be expensive to remove these noxious consequences of indifference to what we share, as opposed to what we own as individuals.

4. The map of metropolis is a crazy quilt of political jurisdictions. It has been cut up, in the spread of urbanization, into cities, counties, towns, townships, boroughs, and villages. Each has its own set of officials, boards, commissions, and councils, and each its own prerogatives and powers. But the major problems of metropolis—transportation, environmental pollution, preservation of open space, housing—do not respect the boundaries of these governments and minigovernments. The Village Board cannot, of itself, solve any of these problems, but it can obstruct their solution in protection of its constituents' special interests.

This fact has led to the overlaying of a second web of special-purpose districts on the map to handle one by one the major metropolitan concerns cited above and others. In most instances, neither the boundaries nor the agendas of these districts overlap. Problems are thus handled piecemeal, rather than in relation to one another; a transportation district, for example, may plan a road through land that a park district had set aside for recreation. Often the voters have no chance to express their views: Many special district boards are appointed, and thus not directly accountable to the citizens.

5. The problems of the great core cities, in particular the older ones, have risen in an almost precisely inverse ratio to the cities' ability to solve them. Many of these cities, to put it bluntly, are steadily going broke.

At the beginning of the New Deal, local governments collected more than half of all tax revenues. Now they collect less than 10 per cent. The enormously efficient federal income tax has become the principal means of raising public monies. Metropolis generates the lion's share of federal revenues: In 1965, two-thirds of the take from the U.S. personal income tax came from the hundred largest metropolitan areas alone (there were 231 in all). After the federal government pays its bills and takes care of such essential national functions as defense (along with some not so essential), metropolis gets back just over 8% of the federal budget in aid. The take-and-give can't be expected to balance, but they should not be this far apart.

The revenue squeeze has become especially acute since World War II. The physical plant of the older cities had been neglected through the depression years and declined still further due to wartime restrictions on domestic spending. At the same time, these cities were feeling the impact of the great internal migration from rural to urban areas, from the South to the North and West. The blacks who came from the farms to the cities crowded into the slums— poverty and racial barriers left them no other choice— creating spreading pockets of public need. The concurrent movement of middleclass population and of economic activity to the suburbs cut away at the core cities' tax base, and thus at their ability to respond.

This aggregate picture—the poor in the cities, the wealth in the suburbs—does not apply uniformly to all metropolitan areas. In 1967, for example, less than half of the poor in the Los Angeles metropolitan area lived in the core city, while in Chicago and New York the figures were 75 and 86 per cent respectively. Yet even in Los Angeles the revenue imbalance is serious enough to have produced a virtual fiscal revolt of property taxpayers. In the older cities it has reached the point of crisis: Newark, in the winter of 1969 was forced to consider closing its libraries to meet its city hall payroll, and a rash of cities, including Philadelphia, were talking of cutting weeks off the school year because of a shortage of funds. The metropolitan pattern cannot be considered healthy, even permanently workable, so long as it concentrates need at the core and lets sources of revenue move outward with no mechanism for recovery.

6. Finally, the range of choices offered by metropolis is not available to all. In metropolis, in fact, the specter of two societies raised by the National Advisory Commission on Civil Disorders is a geographical reality. That is a major reason why there had to be a National Advisory Commission on Civil Disorders.

This, among all the flaws in the metropolitan pattern, is is the one that could prove fatal. The nation has shown that it can tolerate ugliness and waste; suburbia seems willing to live with jurisdictional confusion and the consequent ad-hoc approach to shared problems. Many cope with the deficiencies of the poverty-stricken cities by simply moving away from them. If the people of metropolis are finding the good life outside of the core cities, their decline may be sad but historically inevitable, a painful stage in the evolution of a new form of urbanization.

All this would be at least arguable (if not convincing) were it not for a single fact: Part of the pattern of metropolis is a deliberate racial division that could tear society apart, and, by testimony of the Civil Disorders Commission and others, is beginning to do so.

In postwar years, those who left the city for the suburbs were predominately white. The percentage of white Americans living in the suburbs increased from 26 to 37 from 1950 to 1966. Those who came to the city were predominately Negro. The percentage of black Americans living in the cities increased from 43 to 56 in the same period. Only one statistic remained constant in the 16 years: The percentage of black Americans living in the suburbs stayed at 13.

Economics, of course, had something to do with shaping this pattern. Negro families are three times as likely to be living in poverty as whites in the cities, seven times as likely in the suburbs. The suburbs were not built for, nor do they welcome, the poor. But by no means all of the division was the result of economics. Systematic racial exclusion was part of the system which created metropolis. In the early postwar era, it had the full backing of the government mortgage-insuring agencies: A Federal Housing Administration manual of the period warned that "if a neighborhood is to retain stability, it is necessary that properties shall continue to be occupied by the same racial and social group."

We are only now coming to comprehend the disastrousness of the results. The poor and the minorities of metropolis have been kept in enclaves (first in the core cities, now in the close-in suburbs) of the oldest housing and the oldest, most neglected schools. These enclaves, properly called ghettos, are typically distant from the centers of new job creation. They are places of social distress, where one problem feeds on another and all are intensified by an atmosphere of confinement. They are the places where civil disorder has occurred.

So intractable has been this confinement that some vocal residents of the ghetto have grown frustrated and cynical about the hope of racial integration, of admittance into the mainstream of society, and have adopted separatism as a means of improving their lot. But it can only be a means, not an end. As the Civil Disorders Commission pointed out, separate has always meant unequal for minorities; for the white residents of metropolis, life in a house divided will remain precarious. The end, the goal, must be an end to division, which means opening new options, new mobility, to the minority poor. This goal includes improvement of the present enclaves, helping the blacks to help themselves make the ghettos into viable communities, so that those who choose to stay do not do so at the price of living in blight.

Recently there have been changes in the pattern of metropolitan population movement. In the first six years of this decade, the Negro population of the core cities increased by 376,000 per year. But between 1966 and 1968 the rate of increase dropped to 100,000 and Census Bureau analysts believe it was almost all natural increase —that there had been a virtual halt in black in-migration. In the same two-year period the rate of increase in suburban black population went from 20,000 to 220,000 per year. This change coincided with a rise in black income and employment—yet both the proportion of blacks in poverty and the median black income remained virtually identical in the cities and the suburbs, raising questions of whether the movement to the suburbs was the result of economic progress. It is at least as plausible that it signaled a new era of expansion of suburban ghettos in the inner ring around the core cities, which would not be progress at all.

Still another change involved the white residents of metropolis. Their outmovement from the core city, before 1966, averaged 140,000 a year. In the period 1966-1968, the rate jumped to a half million a year. If the earlier movement to the suburbs was an exercise of preference, this one had the attributes of flight from cities that were becoming centers, not of excellence, but of fear.

METROPOLIS EXPANDED

In 1968, Jerome P. Pickard, in an Urban Land Institute research project, took a long look at the metropolitan future. Pickard projected the shape of American settlement in the year 2000, and found, essentially, that the big urban areas would get much bigger.

Pickard dealt primarily with "major urbanized areas," which he defined as places of 100,000 population or more regardless of relationship to central cities. In 1960, there were 160 such areas in the United States; by 2000 there will be 223 (assuming, as do all of his projections, that present trends continue). They will include places like Yakima, Wash.; Lima, Ohio; and Pascagoula, Miss., whose names in the 1960's are not exactly household words. The total population in these major urbanized areas, 91 million in 1960, will increase to 220.5 million in 2000. In 1960, they were the living places of just over half of all Americans; in 2000, they will accommodate 70 per cent. By then, in fact, more than half the population will live in the 43 urbanized areas of a million or more.

"The projected geographical extent of the great metropolises of 2000," said Pickard with understatement, "is difficult to envision. Fourteen areas will exceed 1,000 square miles in land area (only two did in 1960) ranging *upward to 4,900 square miles in the Los Angeles Basin and 4,300 square miles in New York-Northeastern New Jersey." What he calls a "new dimension" of urbanization will occur through "both the continuous enlargement of the urban fringe and by the merging into the fringe of previously outlying urban areas which are either independent satellites or separated suburban communities." The result will be formation of great continuous urban regions.*

Calmly, Pickard outlined the consequences of this growth. Again given continuation of present trends, growth "will only aggravate and compound present problems of political fragmentation. . . . American urban society may go much further in the direction of technical development, a less personalized society, larger metropolitan masses, and cultural complexity. . . . The concentrated character of future urban regional development will place a great strain upon regional resources: water supply, air, and the land itself. The pollutants generated in such large-scale urban and industrial concentrations may threaten a large segment of the environment, inhabited by the majority of U.S. population. . . ."

Pickard dealt with sheer numbers of people, not kinds of people. Also in 1968, the National Commission on Urban Problems published projections of future population by Patricia Leavey Hodge and Philip M. Hauser which were finer in grain and shorter in range: They covered the period 1960-1985, and included the factors of age and race. They used the Census definition of metropolitan areas, and concluded that, by 1985, these areas will have grown from 113 million people to 178 million.

In the process, the central cities will lose 2.4 million whites and the suburbs will gain 53.9 million; the central cities will gain 10 million nonwhites and the suburbs 4 million. In 1985, then, 70 per cent of the metropolitan whites will be living in the suburbs and 75 per cent of the metropolitan nonwhites in the central cities. The two demographers commented as follows: "The projections vividly portray the geographic fulfillment of the fears expressed by the President's Commission on Civil Disorders —that the American society is becoming an apartheid society. If the geographic separation of white and nonwhite population occurs as projected, America by 1985 would be well on the road toward a society characterized by race stratification along social and economic lines. . . ."

They also added two sobering footnotes: While the over-all population increases 41 per cent, among nonwhites in the central cities the number of school-age youngsters (under 15) will increase 92 per cent—and the "young

workers" (15 to 44) by 112 per cent. The impact on the educational and employment problems of the inner city cannot be statistically projected, only imagined.

Chairman of the National Commission on Urban Problems is former U.S. Senator Paul H. Douglas, who suggested when the population study was made public that it "should be read not as prophecy but as warning." Douglas also said that population growth, in itself, is "an opportunity as well as a challenge." The nature of the opportunity, and ways of using it to improve the nation's environmental and social prospects, are examined in the following two chapters.

THE CONCEPT OF URBANIZATION

Peter Paul

the first comprehensive analysis of American urbanization was published by A. F. Weber in 1899. In it he said, "The process of concentration of population is centralizing in its tendencies; that is the large cities are growing more rapidly than the small cities and absorbing the great bulk of the urban increase." In 1968, the Advisory Commission on Intergovernmental Relations' study of the 1960-1965 net immigration estimates reached the same conclusion: "The lion's share of the population increases will occur in the largest, fastest growing urban areas."

The amount of urbanized land in 1960 was approximately 24,000 square miles; Jerome Pickard projects a requirement for 59,000 square miles of urbanized land by the end of the century if the trends of the past 40 years continue. The additional 35,000 square miles is equivalent in area to the entire state of Indiana.

Still, the total will represent only 2 per cent of the American land area. The problem is in its distribution. Wilderness in Alaska, for example, will afford little benefit to the average New Jersey industrial worker who has to drive beyond the Canadian border before he is out of the suburbs.

The problem is not numbers of Americans. Only the most thickly populated state, New Jersey, with about 800 persons per square mile in 1960, had a density approximating that of Japan, or Belgium, or the Netherlands. With its total resources of available land, the United States can accommodate the increased number of people. The problem is that the people will concentrate in regions where they can share the advantages of urbanization. In the decades ahead, the distribution of urban space will be as severe a concern in America as it is in the world's most densely populated nations.

Modern urbanization can be seen as the product of an industrial system which, in order to increase productivity, subdivided each task into its specialized parts. The large city afforded a concentration of specialists capable of performing increasingly complex functions with rising productivity.

The process has produced an affluent economic system, but its by-product has been an increasing tendency to fragmentation in urban society. Each specialized group acts in terms of its own interests. In the process, natural reactions tend to be overlooked. Pollution occurs because it is nobody's concern; ugliness can be disregarded.

Americans have always associated the city with individual alienation. It is more accurate to say that urbanization and individual alienation spring from common sources, and that the problem must be resolved in an urbanizing society.

Maintaining large urban concentrations involves increasing costs which are both economic and social. The Advisory Commission on Intergovernmental Relations' studies of policies for future growth suggested that diseconomies of scale occurred in larger cities, both for public services and for individuals in maintaining an acceptable standard of living. While the city affords opportunities for those able to meet its demands, it also exacts a high social cost from those not so able. In the large city, poverty and failure become isolated in an environment whose festering discontents breed on each other. The city's power and its disorder are but opposite faces of the urbanizing process.

The city's outward spread has been accelerated by a trend toward lower densities within urbanized areas. Colin Clarke describes the tendency toward lower urban density as a worldwide phenomenon. Gross densities in older city areas were generally around 25,000 persons per square mile; in some parts of the 19th-century city, they were pushed well above 100,000 per square mile (as in New York's Harlem). In few communities or suburban areas are densities much above 10,000 to 12,000 persons per square mile.

Decreased urban density reflects a widespread ability to afford greater amenities of space and nature. But some of the decrease simply reflects waste of land—and waste of public outlays to service a pattern of random development scattered past trapped land. The urban densities which Pickard projects on the basis of past trends are only about a third as great as new community development can afford, even in high-income areas.

Cities have become metropolitan areas. The metropolitan areas have grown together and will continue to do so. The rural space between cities, unaffected by urbanization, will continue to disappear. In the vast urban regions now formed and expanding, all land will respond to forces emanating in the city. America has now entered the era when metorpolitan regions are losing their traditional ability to expand outward: Their boundaries are beginning to touch and merge.

The 1960's marks the decade when Americans became aware of the difference. Jean Gottman described the continuous metropolitan band of the northeastern United States in his monumental study, "Megalopolis." Megalopolis has become a ground in the urban litany. It describes the thrust of future urban growth throughout the country and throughout the world. It also describes an awareness of its nature which did not exist a decade ago.

One need not look farther than the area between Washington and Baltimore to see the result of this phenomenon. Here major activity of expansion is occurring at the "seam of influence" between the two cities, on a line running from Columbia, Laurel, and Fort Meade to Frederick and Annapolis. Major government installations and major private employers are locating where they can draw on the advantages and the labor force of each city.

Behind this merging edge of growth, the by-products of change litter the countryside—worked-out gravel pits and mines; dumps; ill-conceived subdivisions; rotting highway strips drained of their economic blood; leftover towns of an earlier era; and everywhere, yesterday's suburban tract waiting for the forest to grow back as each year chips away at its once salable newness. Land pollution thus will join the pollution of water and air as a phenomenon of the 1970's.

THE NATURE OF SUBURBANIZATION

Suburb implies a unit which is subordinate to the city. It is the physical fact of urban growth beyond the borders of the city, accompanied by political separation from the central city.

The suburban phenomenon began as a socially exclusive one. Upper- and then middle-income families who could afford the costs moved away from the crowded areas of the city center. Today, suburbanization is becoming universal. The suburbs generate employment as well as providing housing.

They always have. Industry has long been a suburban phenomenon. The complex steel mills and railyards of the 19th century frequently had to look for land outside the boundaries of the traditional city. Great land-consuming industries have continued to look to the large tracts of open suburban land for expansion. The automobile permitted industry to be independent of housing. Future fringe development will include employment for people of all occupations and income levels. Suburban employment will be a fundamental force in shaping the future city.

A European observer, G. A. Wissink, suggests that only a portion of suburban development is the result of an effective, stabilized pursuit of better living conditions. Other suburban development lacks the planning which will maintain a stable environment. Some development which occurs outside the city may have been implicitly excluded from the city by its character and land requirements. Some is marginal in nature. Suburban development contains a wide spectrum of elements, some superior, some

37

inferior to those traditionally located in the city.

Outside today's cities and their suburban areas lies the great unbuilt American city, larger in area, perhaps, than the whole urban complex which exists in present time. Its shape is set in the rules by which the game of suburban development is played today. Too frequently, the rules have been used for socially restrictive purposes; too frequently, they have been used to reinforce a senseless fragmentation whose consequences will grow more acute as the physical traces of the city expand outward.

To many, the suburban towns have provided a scale within the vast metropolitan complex in which they can function effectively to project themselves onto their environment. The American promise teaches that citizens should be able to participate in the control of their public affairs. But there must be a balance between the individual's ability to affect his own environment and the need to bind the fractures of urban growth being scattered about the metropolitan landscape together into a just community.

CITY OF COMMUNICATIONS

The traditional concept has regarded the city as a collection of people and forms concentrated into an area of land. It is changing to a concept of the city as a center of communications and of institutional structures which relate to each other.

In megalopolitan regions, the influence of the city is universal. Yet to treat all land as a commodity and to build by present market and regulatory forces alone assures continuing results which are inadequate. The concept is too limited. It is haunted by economic man, a kind of 19th-century stick figure with a very long shadow.

Today, the educational system has had revolutionary impact. The prospects of leisure and affluence are forces that should be shaping the unbuilt America. What is the changing concept of community in the communications-centered city?

Leisure is the time not required for production. John Gardner speaks of this time as giving the opportunity to pursue meaningful goals. Leisure and affluence afford the opportunity to choose among goals and to achieve excellence in their pursuit. He sees these goals as an extension of the highest traditional Americans ideals. The achievement of excellence provides a program for American urbanization.

The physical aspect of urbanization is that of space filling up, of metropolitan regions that have met and can no longer expand outward, of limited space that cannot continue to be littered with disposable commodities called "development." The question is no longer *where* the city will grow but *how*. The concept of urbanization will become nonspatial; its thrust will be toward community and culture.

When the question of how to handle future numbers is resolved, the impact of urbanization can be spread to more places and smaller places. Many places within the extended metropolitan regions and many urban places outside should be able to utilize the economic and technological potential which the United States has to respond to the concept of the communications-centered city.

Beyond the edge of the city where today's suburb trails off into fitful countryside, there is another city larger than any that has been built before. You cannot see it even if you drive off into the cornfields. But it is there, breathing in the silence all around you. It is there in the forces that are already loosed, in the rules you have established, in the adjustments you will make.

Some cherish a hope that it will be exclusive, that it will separate the rich and prosperous would-be beautiful people of suburban America from the teeming masses of the old city's outworn shell. Some build the dream of a provincial America that would separate "them" from "us," that would trade the American Dream for a posh party by the pool away from the city riot. Which America is stirring there in the silence beside you, in the great unbuilt American city?

SOCIAL STRATEGY AND URBAN GROWTH
Harold C. Fleming

the vast numbers of black farm workers who have migrated to the cities—
5.5 million between 1950 and 1966—have brought with them the largest
accumulation of the nation's social deficits ever visited on an identifiable
group. They came from an exploitative agrarian system that denied them
the elementary decencies of life—in income, housing, health, skill development, and education. Like hosts of earlier migrants from other countries,
they crowded into the great urban centers in search of opportunity. But
they found in the slum ghettos an environment at least as destructive, though
in different ways, as the one they had escaped. Thus for many of them the
other side of Jordan proved barren, and the search appears to have ended in
frustration and bitterness.

It is in keeping with the historic role of the cities that they should serve
as collecting points for the dispossessed—in this instance, not foreign immigrants but native Americans whose plight the nation as a whole ignored
for generations. But, in contrast to earlier periods, the cities have lacked
the resources, the ingenuity, and the will to create social mobility for the
newcomers. The old city machines that—with all their faults—provided
patronage, jobs, and case work of a sort to earlier immigrants are virtually
extinct. Racial discrimination has been a formidable added barrier to mobility. More and more industry has decamped to the outlying areas, beyond
the effective reach of public transportation. Coupled with the burgeoning
problems of the physical environment, this is a formula for urban bank-
ruptcy, disorder, and decay.

The manifestations of anger and despair in the ghetto cannot be under-
stood by measuring the material circumstances of its inhabitants against
those of the vanishing Southern sharecropper. However stunted his oppor-

tunities, the citydweller is likely to fare better materially than the marginal farmhand whose every waking moment is a struggle for physical survival. But that very fact has made possible the revolution of rising aspirations, the mounting impatience and rage of many black activists. They do not compare the squalor of the ghetto to the crumbling plantation shack, but to the relative opulence of the nearby white urban and suburban enclaves. And so it is with income, the level of public services, and the quality of life in general in the bleak heart of the metropolis. This is not surprising: Men do not and should not be expected to gauge their well-being by absolute gains over an abysmal past or by the standards of relative misery in far-off places. The poor, no less than the affluent, reckon their status in relation to the general society which surrounds them.

It follows from this, pragmatically as well as ethically, that the necessary goal of social strategy is the equalizing of opportunity, the narrowing of the gap in real choices available to the black and the poor on the one hand, and the white and more affluent on the other. Some have argued that the pursuit of this egalitarian goal is a utopian fallacy. Relative advantage and disadvantage, they maintain, is a permanent feature of human society; therefore, if dissidence and alienation can only be eliminated by equality, we are doomed to failure. But this argument misses the central point, which is how people perceive the causes of inequality. It is one thing to end up on a lower rung of the ladder because of lesser ability, or even bad luck; it is another to be consigned to relative disadvantage at the moment of birth by ancestry or group identity. Caste and class are simply not compatible with the ethical claims of our society.

Defining the goal as equality of choice may serve to dissipate some of the confusion and conflict that now frustrates public discussion of these issues. For many black militants, the term "integration" has become an epithet. It conjures up images of white deceit and broken promises, of tokenism and paternalism, of a continuing campaign to keep the Negro in psychological and political bondage. In the light of past practices, it is not surprising that it should be so. But this is no justification for accepting the simple-minded terms of the debate over "integration" versus "separatism." A real choice between these alternatives is not presently available to the great majority of Negro Americans—or, by extension, to white Americans either. The notion of voluntary separatism becomes a bad joke in the absence of any other alternative.

The fear that salt-and-pepper integration may somehow be forced wholesale upon unwilling blacks and whites is hardly realistic. In a nonauthoritarian society, people cannot be manipulated like pawns on a chessboard. Those who prefer to live in proximity to others of like racial, ethnic, cultural, or economic background (so long as they are not fanatically purist) can accomplish their aim well enough in an open society without resort to violence or officially ordained apartheid. The relevant questions are whether and how we are to achieve a truly open society in the United States. If we can find affirmative answers to these questions, we need not worry unduly about black opposition to a policy that offers Negroes as free a choice of residence as whites now enjoy.

Such reasoning is philosophically satisfying, at least for those of liberal bent, but the harsh reality is that racial separatism, whether espoused by blacks or whites, is today in no jeopardy whatever. Unless there is a large-scale mobilization of national determination and resources to prevent it, what is in store is a vast increase in de facto segregation. One can find a ray of hope, however, in considering the dimensions of change and innovation that will be demanded, irrespective of racial factors, by prospective population growth and technological development. Major social reform benefiting minorities tends to occur when the society as a whole is in ferment. Some of the chief (albeit far from adequate) economic gains made by Negro Americans came during the Depression, World War II, and to a lesser extent, the Korean War. In recent and more complacent years, however, many of the relatively affluent along with resentful lower-middle-income whites have come to view demands made on behalf of the black poor as a threat to their own interests. This resistant majority has seen as the problem the disadvantaged minorities themselves rather than malfunctions of the social and economic institutions of the society.

Current projections augur a possible change in this situation. Pressure is already mounting for federal rescue of local and state budgets in the populous industrial areas; property and sales tax and other non-federal sources of revenue are reaching the point of no more return; many suburban areas are beginning to realize that unplanned development, traffic congestion, and environmental pollution are not central city monopolies. The pressure on educational facilities from kindergarten through college, including the rising enrollments and costs of higher education, alarms upwardly mobile whites at least as much as lower-income blacks. Projected population growth can only intensify these problems and generate new demands on government to facilitate their solution. To predict the responses to these demands and to prescribe the social component of each prospective new policy is far beyond the ambition of this chapter. But it is possible to indicate some of the opportunities for social innovation that are inherent in the situation:

1. *Flexibility of new systems.* It is a well documented fact that social change comes more easily in new than in old, established situations. For example, segregation died hard on the Southern railroads but was never practiced on airplanes and not for long in air terminals. Stable housing desegregation has been most readily achieved in new developments where the requisite effort was made from the outset. Enforcement of desegregation requirements of Title VI of the 1964 Civil Rights Act has been far more successful in hospitals, many of which were newly covered through participation in Medicare, than in public schools, which were long accustomed to federal aid. Similar experience can be cited in the fields of employment and union practices. By the same token, new patterns of settlement can incorporate

new principles of rational social and economic organization with far less opposition than a reversal of old patterns encounters. But this opportunity can be realized only if it is recognized and exploited from the very inception of new policies and programs.

2. *Population growth.* The magnitude of expectable population increase argues for the use of powerful incentives and deterrents to promote workable economic and racial balance. If the present concentrations of racial and economic groups were a stable phenomenon, we might conceivably rely on existing processes to bring about gradual advancement and equalization of opportunity for residents of the ghetto. But the dynamics of natural increase, not to mention the still undepleted reservoirs of rural poverty, rule out such a laissez-faire approach. The consequence would be unbearably swollen enclaves of disadvantage, discontent, and chronic disorder.

Therefore, new national policies aimed at channeling population growth per se must also seek to make possible diversification by race and income. Federal and state policies designed to facilitate the development of new towns and accelerated growth centers should embody requirements for housing and job opportunities for low- as well as middle- and higher-income families. Government contractors and government installations themselves should be required to see that housing is available within a reasonable commuting distance for nonwhite and lower-income workers. Block grants to states or localities should carry with them the firm condition that allocations proportionate to need must be made to low-income people.

It should be observed in passing that too little attention has been given to what constitutes a socially desirable mix under what circumstances.

Study of this question deserves high priority. Meanwhile, it is probably safe to say that the over-all area within which diverse groups will be accommodated is likely to be relatively large—more on the order, say, of the high school attendance area than the block or the neighborhood. Such a pattern would conform to the familiar tendency of families of like background to cluster rather than scatter in buckshot fashion. If this proves to be the case, special attention must be given to school districting that will provide for racial balance at the elementary as well as secondary level.

3. *Population mobility.* The high rate of mobility of the nation's population makes it a matter of urgent national interest to establish uniform standards for welfare, education, and food distribution. Under existing policies, the accident of geography determines how adequate a welfare payment (if any) a destitute citizen may receive, the kind and amount of surplus food (if any) an impoverished and hungry family is entitled to, and the objective quality of schooling a child is offered. The gross inequalities that result are obviously inhumane; but they are also, less obviously, productive not merely of localized but of national distemper. Indeed, the current urban crisis is in large part the result of local discriminations too long tolerated by an apathetic nation.

In an era of unprecedented mobility, poverty and ignorance are mobile too. The individual who is denied the opportunity to learn and develop because of the prejudice or backwardness of one locality today will likely be a burden on another locality tomorrow. A child in South Carolina who is damaged physically and perhaps even mentally for want of adequate nutrition today may be the ward of New York or Illinois or California tomorrow. The

impoverished family that receives trifling or nonexistent welfare payments at the whim of a local official in a nonurban area can hardly be blamed for swelling the welfare rolls in a city that pays perhaps six times as much. No nation that cares about minimal equity for its citizens and a rational distribution of its population should tolerate such abuses of local discretion in the name of federalism.

As the time rapidly nears when states and localities can no longer meet their rising welfare and educational costs and must seek greater federal subvention, long overdue reform is in order. Whether the welfare system is continued in its present form or in combination with some type of income maintenance, increased federal funding should assure uniform benefits in all parts of the country. The crisis in school financing offers a similar opportunity to reduce the enormous inequalities that now exist between states, districts, and even schools within the same district.

4. *Metropolitanwide programming.* Any rational policy of urbanization must seek to bring into being a variety of mechanisms that can operate effectively across the maze of local jurisdictions. State instruments, for example, with authority to assemble land and determine its pattern of use, to provide incentives for desired types of housing, to plan transportation networks, to promote economic development, and the like, would obviously have great influence on social factors as well. But there is no assurance that this influence would be used consistently or constructively in the absence of properly directed and mandated national policies. Without them, local veto power would doubtless continue to block construction of low-income housing, model cities programs, and the whole range of interventions aimed at improving the status of the poor and the black; moreover, there is reason to assume that many of the state governments themselves would be unsympathetic to social change.

The essential element, therefore, is the leverage of the major federal financial assistance that would be an indispensable part of this process. Only if such assistance is conditioned on broadening the choices of the minority poor will an urbanization policy be rational in execution as well as conception. It may be argued that this degree of "federal interference" is politically infeasible. This assumes it will be impossible to gain broader public acceptance than now exists for the proposition that the national interest is so severely threatened by social as well as environmental problems that only a national strategy for both will do. If such pessimism is justified, there is no hope for rational urbanization.

5. *The central city.* Any rational strategy of urban growth must link the need for new growth areas with the need to alleviate the critical problems of the central cities. In the absence of such a comprehensive approach, efforts to restructure and revitalize the cities have faced insuperable obstacles. For example, urban renewal ideally should have come to maturity when people in the older, blighted areas were moving upward economically and socially,

and outward physically. Thus large tracts of inner-city land would have become available, relatively painlessly, for clearance and diversified development. But the facts of urban life have been less and less congenial to this concept of renewal. The increase of the black poor in the central city has put a premium on rehabilitation and replacement of low- and moderate-income housing in renewal areas. Relocation, never likely to be a popular process, has come to be widely viewed as racist and inhumane—a problem made worse by the inability of the program to operate across local governmental boundaries. Those types of renewal that would make the central city attractive to business and industry and to the white middle class have come to be regarded as inimical to the minority poor.

The social strategy here suggested would make possible a more favorable set of circumstances. If it became practicable and desirable for enough lower-income Negroes to rent or buy in the outlying areas of new growth, the need and demand for low-income housing in the central city would decline. Clearance and relocation would need no longer carry the stigma of "Negro removal." As economic and racial balance was achieved in new towns and other new growth areas, so would it become possible again in the central city.

The key, of course, is timing. Planning, the deployment of resources, and redevelopment in the central city must be synchronized with new development and population movement to the outlying areas. At all events, the glamor of the new-town approach must not be allowed to eclipse the prime objective of recreating and reinvigorating the central city.

6. *Self-interest.* The fact that there will presumably be benefits for many Americans of different backgrounds in the new urbanization will also help make social innovation more acceptable. One of the roots of opposition to progressive social change is the widespread conviction that the minority poor can advance only at the expense, socially as well as economically, of others in the society. Our public policies have not been notably successful in dispelling this apprehension by fusing ethical and self-interested motives. The design of new urban policies will, hopefully, do better by this simple psychological principle.

Direct subsidies to low-income families, unlike grudging welfare payments and monolithic public housing, can enlist the energies of the marketplace in the service of upward mobility of the poor. Our studies of fair housing indicate that whites or nonwhites who are indifferent or even somewhat hostile to integration in principle will readily accept desegregated living if it offers unusual advantages of price or convenience. A rational policy of urban growth will have much to offer to all of us, not only as homeowners but as businessmen and industrialists, blue-collar and white-collar workers, builders and developers, and public officials at all levels of government. The carrot, then, rather than the less effective stick, can and should become the main inducement for the creation of democratic patterns of living.

47

THE CHOICE OF A PLACE TO LIVE is influenced by as many preferences and prejudices as there are people. Some choose the city, because it is a center of culture, or because they like the excitement of its night life, or even because they like the sense of urbanity in tall buildings broken by occasional, managable, pleasurable fragments of nature.

The city offers an endless variety of ways and places to spend one's spare time, one's own time, whether a fe minutes sitting in a downtown plaza, a Sunday in the park, an afternoon at the bocci court.

It's big-league sports—and big-league cocktail parties.

The city is a place to make money and a place to spend it, or just to window shop. It is the marketplace.

There is, for many, a magnetism to the city. Part of the magnetism may be its sheer size and compaction; part its sense of stateliness, of a gracious past; part the chance to touch institutions that are larger than one's self.

Others come to regret their choice of the city, or are there because they have no choice. In the shadow of its grandeur there is decay and despair. The constant press of worries about where to live or where to work, the constant press of other people, can become unbearable in these hard and treeless streets.

Growing up in this part of the city, survival is itself an accomplishment. These streets are also streets of fear.

Some choose small-town life, for reasons that are obvious from this photograph: peace, breathing spa

eness to more nature than an urban park can provide.

Life here is close-knit, quiet. There is no need to dress up to be with friends, except on special occasions. Here the flag flies; here the old virtues still prevail.

But here too is poverty as bad as in the worst streets of the city. Opportunity, and hope, have passed this villag

And so they leave the shacks for the city—not because they like it better, but because they need more than the land will ever again yield, or want their children to know more of the world than can be learned in the wooden walls of a single room.

The suburbs have become, in postwar years, the Great American Compromise—for those who can afford them. Their promise is a combination of urbanity (just 45 minutes away) and the greenery of the small town. The greenery must be mowed, of course, and much of it winds up paved over to accommodate that basic suburban appliance, the private car.

There has been a great deal of generalizing about suburbia, but only one generalization has proved durable: A great many people seem to like it there. Suburbs can be so well designed that the houses seem to grow like the trees from wooded land; or they can be thrown up among the poles and wires of a denuded site. Time and people make a difference. This is Levittown, N.Y., the way it looked when built and the way it looks today.

Even those who like suburbia pay a price. It can be a long drive to work, to shop, to sample the excitement of the city (just 45 minutes away). The price, and the distances, have been increased by the planless, heedless way suburbia has spread. It is still spreading.

PLANNING AND PRECEDENTS

the word planning has two major overtones: a sense of purpose and a sense of future. These are two qualities that have been noticeably lacking in the process of American urbanization. So far we have been willing, by and large, to see the shape of the nation be determined by a random accretion of individual decisions, with little regard for the end result. We have been building urban America as if there were no tomorrow.

It doesn't have to be that way. There is nothing in our history or traditions which says the nation cannot take a hand in its future, cannot decide what it wants to be and how to get there. Others do: We are all but alone among the major democracies in our permissiveness toward the urban development process, in our planless approach to growth.

Planning itself is a process, one that injects a sense of future, of consequences, into the making of day-to-day development decisions. The Regional Plan Association of New York, in a set of proposals for the future of the nation's most populous metropolitan area, made the point explicit: "The regional plan is not a precise blueprint of everything that should be built mile by mile. It is a framework of basic principles which can be applied over the years when development decisions are to be made. Nothing will happen just from publication of the plan. But a great deal happens when a regional-plan principle is laid alongside a prospective public program or private investment so the public can judge the long-term effects."

It is an apt description of the function *of the planning process in relation to metropolitan growth. The association goes on to define other qualities required of a plan for metropolis:*

Scope. *The association's plan (one of two it has drawn for the New York region 37 years apart) deals with "what man will build and reserve unbuilt over the coming generation— homes and apartments, factories and offices, highways and railroads, schools and colleges, stores, museums, theaters, parks. Where people build, what they build, how they build affect all of the urban problems that fill today's newspapers: opportunities for the poor, relations between Negroes and whites, smog, traffic jams. They also affect the abiding issues that do not make headlines: man's relationship to nature, conditions that promote a good society, the form of a great civilization."*

Thus, the association continues, "the plan that begins with buildings also gets into questions of costs and values, taxes and government, welfare and recreation, jobs and health care." The stuff of planning is land and development. The purpose of planning is to improve the lives of people.

Scale. *The association's plan takes in some 12,000 square miles in and around New York City, including parts of New Jersey and Connecticut, an area more than 10 times the size of the presently defined metropolis. It chose to deal with this larger area "because its parts are closely related in jobs, housing, and transportation," or will be in the generation ahead.*

In support of making such a big plan, the association points out that "a firm locating a plant or office first decides to locate it somewhere in the region and then looks for the best place within the region. Similarly, a person moving his family to a job in the region is likely to look in any of dozens of towns and villages—even several counties—for the right place to live. So it is almost a single housing market as well. The price of a piece of land, then, is related to the value of land throughout the region, and major highways are located as part of a regional system. In these and other ways, the region is a unified place and must be planned as a whole."

The regional plan, the association says, does not replace the need for counties and municipalities to plan individually; rather, "it provides a view of what is happening and could happen all around them, allowing each to plan more realistically for itself." At the other end of the scale, there are problems which the region, no matter how well it plans, cannot solve for itself. The association argues for the

states to assume a greater share of educational costs, and for the federal government to pay more of the bill for services dealing with the national problem of poverty. Similarly, it says (cautiously) that the region probably can accommodate the 11 million additional people expected by 2000. Beyond that, it calls for à study of national policies to stem further growth or divert it elsewhere.

Problems. *The association bases its plan on a careful diagnosis of the deficiencies in present patterns of growth. Development is covering over green space. There is a spreading pattern of segregation (the black and Puerto Rican population of New York City is 30 per cent, that of Newark 60 per cent, that of the region's fringes 7 per cent). Unskilled jobs are moving outward where housing is unavailable to those who might fill them; white-collar jobs are clustered in the centers, but white-collar workers live in the fringe. The supply of new housing is limited, even for middle-income families. Those living on the fringe lack community focus, do not enjoy "urban advantages" such as cultural facilities or hospitals large enough to provide broad medical skills. Public transportation is either nonexistent or overcrowded and uncomfortable; highways are congested; traffic jams are now appearing in the sky.*

If some residents of the region are not now seriously inconvenienced by these problems, the association warns that their children will be. The "city lover" contemptuous of the suburbs will find that his children won't be able to fit into the city; the resident of a close-in suburb who feels he has the best of two worlds will find that his children will have to go ever farther outward in search of a place to live.

Goals. *The plan's specific proposals are meant to achieve a set of ambitious ends. In the association's words, the plan "affirms the city's function: bringing people together. But it accepts the suburban value of a one-family house on its own lot for most families with children. It proposes that each of the region's residents have both a small local community and a large, metropolitan sized community. . . . It provides for a much wider choice of jobs, housing, goods, services, activities, and friends than man has ever had before, particularly enlarging these choices for the poor and minority groups. . . . And it issues a call for man to live in greater harmony with nature even in a huge urban region."*

The means to these ends are closely tied to the particular circumstances of the New York region: In outline, the association proposes a clustering of administrative and community facilities into two dozen cores within the region, joined by public transportation and surrounded by high-

density housing for a variety of income groups (the association likens the housing pattern to iron filings attracted to a magnet). It calls for immediate public purchase of all open space that the region will need at full growth, and for a five-step fight against environmental pollution.

But the plan is not cited here for its specifics. Rather, it is offered as a prototype of the kind of planning—in breadth of concern, in scale, in objectives—needed to make positive uses of metropolitan growth. Unfortunately, it is typical of the best of American planning in another way as well: There is, at present, no way to see that it is carried out. The Regional Plan Association is a voluntary organization

which attempts, with high skill and some success, to make its proposals effective through a continuous program of communications among public officials and citizens in the New York area. There is no corresponding public planning body with authority to establish principles to guide the future of the region, much less one with the teeth to make them stick. The same vacuum prevails in nearly every American metropolis.

There are two parts to the problem, the first of which is scale. Planning as such is carried on by a variety of bodies at all levels of jurisdiction: states, metropolitan planning commissions and councils of government, special-purpose

77

districts, counties, municipalities. Since 1954, in fact, the federal government has offered planning assistance and incentives that have steadily broadened the scale of the planning unit.

But plans are dependent for realization on the use of public powers over land use and development. These powers, in this country, are principally zoning ordinances, which determine the nature of development allowed on particular zones of land (residential, commercial, industrial, etc.); and subdivision regulations which determine the direction of development by saying where and how new streets, utilities, and building plots are laid out. "With almost no exceptions," the American Society of Planning Officials said in a report to the National Commission on Urban Problems, "these two legal devices are enactments of the local government having jurisdiction over the area controlled. That is, zoning and subdivision control are almost always the responsibility and prerogative of a village or a city and not of the county or state in which the community is located."

The meaning is that all manner of metropolitan plans can be and are being made, but the powers required to carry them out are held by the smallest units of government. These powers, to say the least, often are used in a self-serving way: "Action by a local government in its own best interest is often against the best interest of its neighbors or of the metropolitan region as a whole," says the American Society of Planning Officials report. A locality which zones for large-lot development to keep itself economically homogeneous, to cite but one example, is contributing directly to the concentration of the poor and minorities, and the best-laid metropolitan housing plan can do nothing about it. Whatever the scale of the planning unit, the scale of decision-making—upon which the planning process depends—does not match the boundaries of metropolitan problems.

Moreover, as the Regional Plan Association pointed out in its treatment of the New York area's future, we are moving toward a point where the best way to handle metropolitan population growth is not to let it happen—to divert it elsewhere, or stem it at the source by improving the environment and economy of smaller communities. This requires planning at the state and national scales, for which there is little precedent in this country but ample precedent abroad. Great Britain, France, the Netherlands, the Scandinavian countries—all have taken a direct hand in land and population deployment in the face of urbanization, and all can point to examples of orderly growth that contrast sharply with the American metropolitan ooze.

The second major difficulty with the present system is that public powers in the field of development, of urbanization, are essentially negative. Even when not used defensively, zoning, subdivision regulations, and the other forms of development control are attuned to preventing evil rather than encouraging good. They are poorly suited to a concept of planning that tries to put growth to positive use —to establish objectives and move toward them, decision by decision, with a sense of purpose.

This concept of planning is best described by example. One approach to it was described by planner John W. Reps of Cornell University in a recent address to his colleagues.

"I propose," said Reps," "that land at the urban fringe which is to be developed for urban uses should be acquired by a public agency." (Pause for loud gasp by audience.) "Acquisition, in fact, should run well ahead of anticipated need and include the purchase or condemnation of idle or agricultural land well beyond the present urban limits. The public agency, therefore, should be given territorial jurisdiction which includes not only the present central city and the surrounding suburbs but a wide belt of undeveloped land.

"Land scheduled for early development," he continued, "should be designed in detail, conforming to a general, comprehensive, and long-range metropolitan growth plan. The public agency, directly or indirectly, should install all street and utility improvements and should identify and retain all sites needed for such public facilities as parks, schools, and other neighborhood and community needs. The remaining land should then be disposed of to private builders by sale or lease, the aggregate price to reflect full acquisition and improvement costs but no profit. The terms of the sale or lease should include adequate safeguards to insure development only in conformity to the detailed plans prepared for the areas."

Reps acknowledged that such an approach, on first hearing, might seem radical, but pointed out that the right of public land acquisition had been upheld by the courts for less compelling public purposes than the shaping of urban growth. On second look, in fact, there are elements of the Reps proposal that are very much in keeping with American tradition as well as law. Private enterprise would do most of the building, and, in fact, would be assured a steady and probably less expensive supply of land on which to build. Among private interests, only land speculators would be the losers. Public investment would be no higher than in the normal course of unplanned peripheral growth, and land for public facilities cheaper to acquire. The price *of public investment, in fact, would be partially offset by the public agency's return for site improvements, now often lost. The price of the land itself to the public agency also would be returned through sale or leases; the entire operation, Reps suggests, could operate on a self-replenishing revolving fund.*

It has been done this way in America. Reps offered the following intriguing precedent:

"A decision was once made that a major project of urban development should be undertaken, that the public interest dictated this should occur on vacant land, and that a careful plan should be prepared to guide this growth. It was no small project. The area involved was enormous— more than 5,000 acres of land. All this land was in private ownership. The owners were speculatively inclined. Most of them yearned to enrich themselves out of this project.

"Largely as the result of the remarkable vision of two men, this entire site was acquired by a public agency. Both men knew from long and immediate experience the prevailing conditions of this country's land market as well as anyone before or since. Both were large landowners themselves and were ardent supporters of political democracy and a free enterprise economy. Yet both adopted the position—and acted accordingly—that only if the land to be developed came entirely into public ownership could a comprehensive urban plan be carried out.

"After the site was acquired and the plan completed, whole blocks as well as individual building sites were sold for development subject to controls over the character of the buildings. Land for streets, squares, open spaces, and public buildings was retained for eventual community use. The result was what is still the most notable city planning project in the United States and ranks with the best in the world."

The project was the city of Washington, D.C.; the two men were George Washington and Thomas Jefferson. Other precedents for planning, from our own history and from the postwar experience of Great Britain, are offered in the following chapters.

AMERICA'S NEGLECTED TRADITION
Carl Feiss

There is no part of the Great American tradition, no part of our history more dynamic, than the settlement of the New World and its pioneering expansion into the wilderness. The story has been told and retold countless times by historians and novelists; each time there is found some new and fascinating element in the saga of people and events which adds to our national pride. It is a pride not only in our adventurous forefathers, but in their extraordinary creative ability.

However, there is one part of the total accomplishment which is all too little known. This is the story of the planned settlements, the new communities, designed with idealism and imagination by the settlers in the New World, who wished to build permanent new homes and better communities than those which they left behind in Holland, Spain, England, and France.

The people who conquered the New World were a mixed bag of buccaneers, real estate promoters, and idealists. Their descendants are still with us; the mixture today is just as competitive as it was 300 years ago. But the story told here concerns just one ingredient in the bag, the strong chain of idealism which connected those who planned our first human settlements. For the design and construction of well-planned new towns or communities in carefully selected locations by both public and private enterprise is an important and integral part of the great American tradition.

While much of the primeval wilderness has been converted through the years to urban wilderness, in our history we can find basic principles of planning and design of urban places to satisfy the physical and psychological needs of people. The destruction of our forests, the eroding of our lands, the pollution of our waters, the building of shack towns and tenement cities were not part of the settlement policies of our more idealistic fore-fathers. For instance, part of the brilliant plan for Savannah by General Oglethorpe in 1784 was the establishment of the "Trustees' Gardens" specifically laid out for the study of botany, horticulture, and agronomy to aid the several planned settlements designed by the general. The preservation of open space within and at the edge of planned pioneer communities is a constant source of wonder, since so many of these communities were built at the edge of, or in the middle of, a vast wilderness of open space.

Perhaps the reason for this care and foresight was that many of our fore-fathers came from overcrowded medieval cities with all too little open space and too few opportunities to enjoy nature. They were also influenced by some of the great new Renaissance planning efforts which were opening up plazas, public squares, and gardens, sometimes in the center and other times at the edges of the medieval cities. Regardless of whether these efforts were the inspiration, or whether it was born new in the new environ-

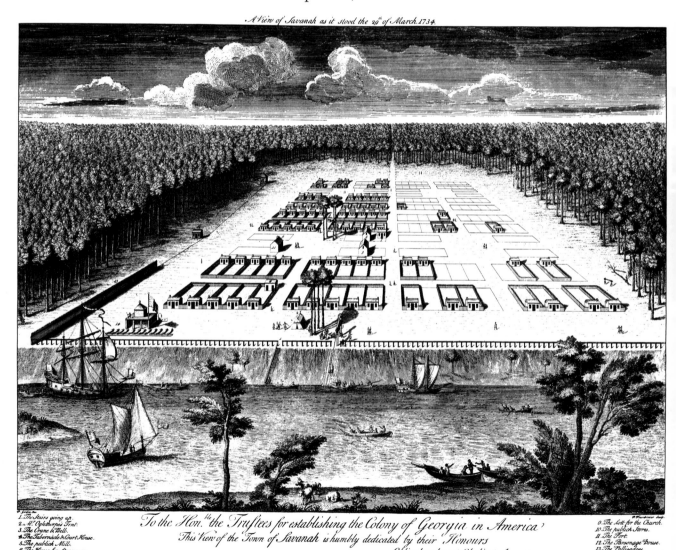

A View of Savanah as it stood the 29th of March. 1734.

1. The Stairs going up.
2. Mr. Oglethorpes Tent.
3. The Crane & Bell.
4. The Tabernacle & Court House.
5. The publick Mill.
6. The House for Strangers.
7. The publick Oven.
8. The draw Well.

To the Honble the Trustees for establishing the Colony of Georgia in America
This View of the Town of Savanah is humbly dedicated by their Honours
Obliged and most Obedient Servant
VÜE de Savanah dans la Georgie.   Peter Gordon

9. The Lott for the Church.
10. The publick Store.
11. The Fort.
12. The Personage House.
13. The Pallisadoes.
14. The Guard House and Battery of Cannon.
15. Hutchinsons Island.

The squares of Savannah, each with its own identity, remain as remnants of the city's earliest plan.

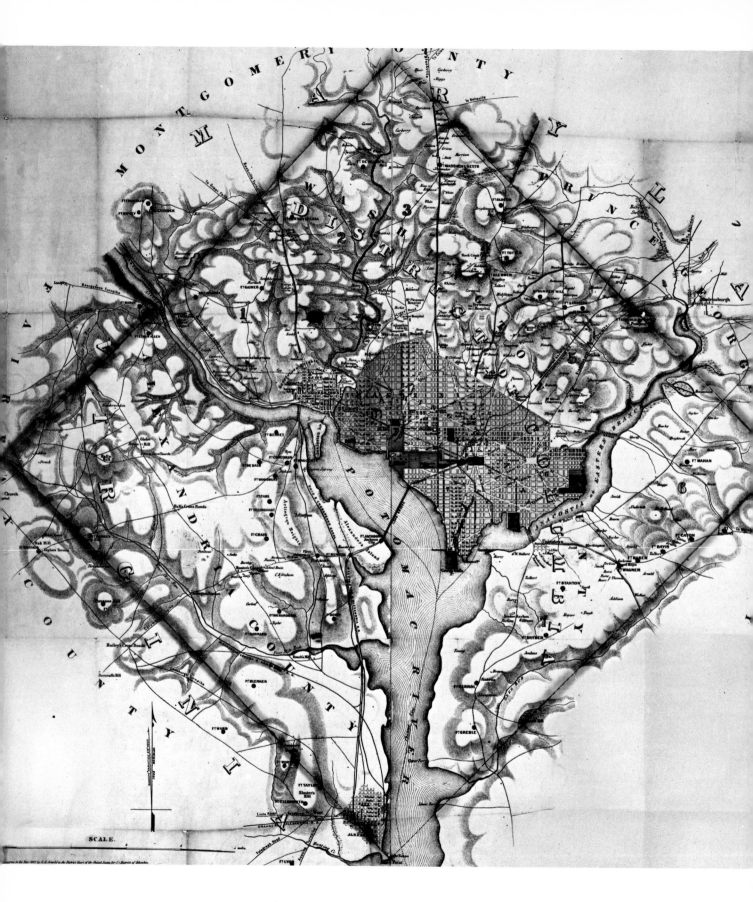

84

ment, the planned new towns in the Americas contained many elements of praiseworthy design.

Many new cities that were built in what is now the United States were badly planned and badly designed, of course. Bad site selection, bad planning, and bad development, including slum conditions, grew hand in hand with the good. For a period of some hundred years after the Civil War, in fact, bad urban design superseded the good, which fell by the wayside with only sporadic attempts to pick it up again. We are still in this bleak period of urban nondesign.

The results of this faltering can be seen in the federally built city of Washington, D.C., carefully and beautifully designed by L'Enfant under the eagle eyes of Presidents Washington and Jefferson in the latter part of the 18th century. When the expansion of the city went beyond the outer limits of the original design, the principles of the plan were abandoned. Washington is surrounded by typical late 19th and early 20th century chaos, just as though no example had been set by L'Enfant in the central city. In the vast new suburban growth of megalopolis, there is little evidence that today's urban builders recognize a planned area when they see it, let alone know relevant American history.

"LAWS OF THE INDIES"

The French, English, and Dutch, the main colonizers of North America, left the policy of settlement design largely in the hands of the individual colonizers holding royal grants or patents. They also gave the individual immigrant groups such as the Pilgrim Fathers in New England and the Massachusetts Bay Company license to do pretty much what they pleased in the way of arranging the affairs of the colonies. It is amazing how well they did.

The Spaniards took another course: After early and not too successful free-wheeling of some of their expeditionary forces, they decided that a strict and orderly settlement policy for new towns was required. Therefore, in 1573, King Philip the Second issued the earliest planning legislation in the Americas, the "Laws of the Indies." These laws were based on careful analysis of the successes and failures of earlier colonies. They "established uniform standards and procedures for planning of towns and their surrounding lands as well as for all other details of colonial settlement," John Reps wrote in his book "Town Planning in Frontier America."

The "Laws of the Indies" went into detail on site selection for a new town, on street layout, on location of public squares, plazas, and important buildings. This remarkable set of documents influenced the design of several North American cities, including St. Augustine, Pensacola, Los Angeles, and San Diego.

Similar legislation began appearing early in the development of the original colonies. When Jamestown, Va., was to be enlarged in 1662, the legislature passed an "Act for Building a Towne." According to Reps, a series

85

of New Towne Acts in Virginia and Maryland designed to shape and encourage settlement were passed from 1662 through 1706. Twenty sites for new towns, each of 15 acres, were designated under Virginia laws; 57 sites of 100 acres each were designated under a Maryland Act of 1683. While many of these towns no longer exist, several formed the basis for modern cities in the two states.

Most of the earliest new towns in North America lacked the design quality and distinction of the contemporary Spanish examples. It was not until Francis Nicholson, lieutenant governor of Virginia, secured the passage of a second general Town Planning Act in Virginia in 1691 that a change in quality of design began. He appears to have been responsible in large part for the layout of Annapolis in 1695. He was undoubtedly responsible for the 1699 legislation in Virginia establishing the new town of Williamsburg and specifying elements of its design. The distinctive plan of Williamsburg grew out of Nicholson's acquaintance with the brilliant designs of Sir Christopher Wren and John Evelyn for the rebuilding of London after the great fire of 1666.

Undoubtedly, the most ambitious and the most successful of the early American urban settlement schemes was that for the new city of Philadelphia, designed and laid out by William Penn in 1683. Philadelphia extended two miles in length from the Delaware River to the Schuylkill and had a breadth of one mile. Four of the five squares of the original plan were the first designated public parks in any city in the United States. William Penn also drew up a metropolitan development plan involving some 10,000 acres outside of the city of Philadelphia, laying out rural settlements and agricultural villages, and designed a road system to connect them.

New community settlements in the early Colonial period of New England began on a significant scale after the establishment of the Massachusetts Bay Colony in the early 1630's. Numerous new villages were laid out with common fields and common pasture lands. The village green, the town center, usually was the site of the church, the meetinghouse, and other public buildings, and was frequently used as a parade ground for the local militia. The most formal of these new settlements was New Haven, laid out in 1638 as a square of nine large blocks. The central block was green, 825 feet on a side, the largest in all of New England.

One characteristic of the 17th and 18th century New England villages was that the owner of lots in the center of a community also owned agricultural acreage at its outskirts. This significantly limited the expansion of the village and is one of the reasons why so many have retained their early dimension to this day. A permanent greenbelt of farm lands and wood lots not only restricted the urban growth pattern, but provided a continuing agricultural economic base which has served well through the centuries.

A natural result of this land-use pattern was that, as populations grew, it was necessary for younger sons and other members of large families who did not inherit land or industry to look elsewhere for their own homes and

86

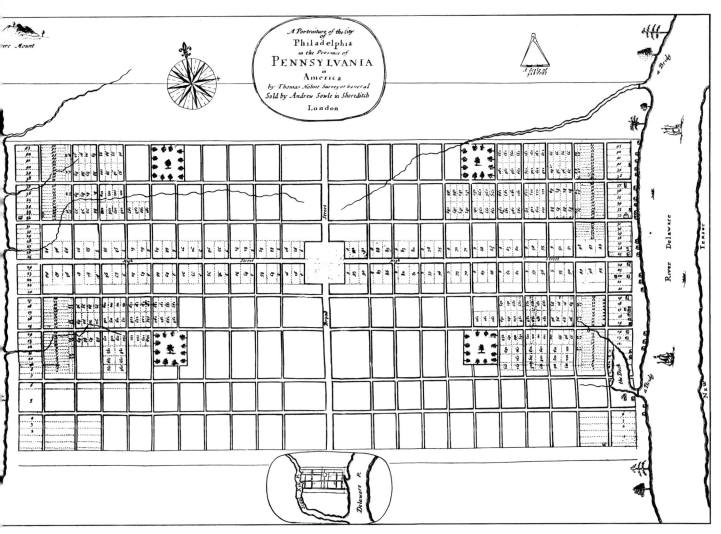

A Portraiture of the City of Philadelphia in the Province of PENNSYLVANIA in America by Thomas Holme Surveyor General Sold by Andrew Soule in Shoreditch London

livelihood. It was not unusual for a settlement to establish a new-town colony of its own farther west. Several of the Massachusetts Bay settlements colonized early Connecticut river towns, one of which was Windsor. In 1793 Windsor was responsible for colonizing the planned city of Cleveland, Ohio, in the Connecticut Western Reserve.

When Ipswich, Mass., a beautifully planned fishing and farm village of the late 17th century, could no longer house and feed its population, it sent out its own colony by ox team and Conestoga wagon to settle on a site found for it by the Ohio Company of Associates. Under the direction of General Rufus Putnam, a brilliant town planner in his own right, the colony built the city of Marietta, Ohio, which opened the first Sunday school and day school in the Northwest Territory in the winter of 1788-89. For those of us today who are concerned with the question of extraterritorial rights for our crowded cities, and in the possibility of the establishment of new towns or settlements to decant overpopulated urban centers, it is interesting to note that these activities were common practice both during Colonial times and in the early days of the Republic.

The most famous of the early and mid- 18th century planned communities in the United States, besides Philadelphia, are Savannah and New Orleans. Historic Savannah, a two-square mile area in the center of the modern city, was laid out by General Oglethorpe on the basis of a remarkable open-space plan. The basic module for the plan, called the ward, consisted of an open square, local streets, and lots for public and private construction. The original six wards finally multiplied to 21 just before the Civil War. After that the city seems to have forgotten the advantage of the ward plan; its further development largely followed the standard gridiron system.

Unlike Savannah, New Orleans was designed as a unit in 1722. The plan of New Orleans, although French in origin, is similar to the plan for St. Augustine: a walled city, with a centered parade facing on the open water and a church facing on the open square opposite. There are also similarities between the French plan for Mobile and the Spanish plan for Pensacola, each with a central fortification surrounded by an open space and then surrounded by a grid plan. Undoubtedly, both geographic proximity and cultural interests influenced the designs of these cities.

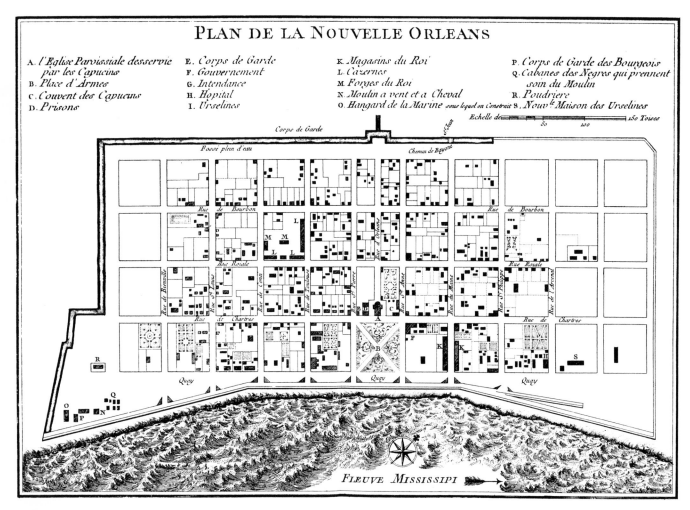

Jackson Square is a legacy of the original plan for New Orleans.

As New England moved west and developed new settlements, it joined forces with the New Yorkers. In the late 18th and early 19th centuries, a series of delightful small cities grew along the Hudson and the Mohawk Rivers on the route of the Erie Canal. In the meantime, and following in the same generally western direction, expansion from Pennsylvania and Virginia crossed the Appalachians and floated down the Ohio. Thomas Jefferson himself designed settlements in Kentucky and Indiana. The plan of Washington, D.C., which had become widely known in the early 1800's. influenced the design of the new city of Buffalo in 1804 and the new capital of Indiana, Indianapolis, in1821.

The last important planned city in the United States before the Civil War was Salt Lake City, laid out in 1848 by Brigham Young for some 8,000 Mormon migrants. The plan of Salt Lake City was based on the plan of the city of Zion given to the Elders of the Mormon Church in 1833 by Joseph

BIRD'S EYE VIEW OF

SALT LAKE CITY

UTAH TERRITORY
1870.

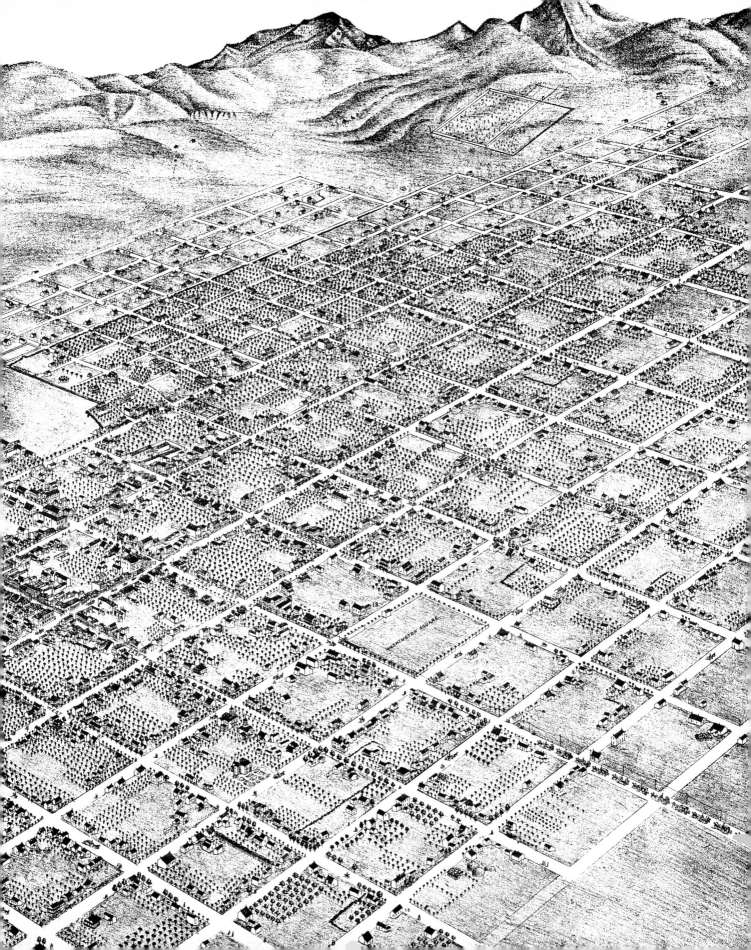

Salt Lake City owes its broad boulevards to the planning abilities of Brigham Young.

Smith, which also served as the basis for the many Mormon settlements in Utah and other parts of the Southwest. Brigham Young was an excellent city planner. Salt Lake City was laid out with exceptionally broad streets. The plan was accompanied by many regulatory measures common to new community design a hundred years later, including setback lines for buildings and a street tree planting program.

Salt Lake City was the culmination of the nearly 100 years of building of planned religious utopias. This movement began with the founding of Bethlehem, Pa., in 1741 by the Moravians as the first of several planned new communities which they settled in various parts of the central East Coast. They were followed by dozens of religious and other utopian movements interested in building a better world, and therefore better cities. A few of these idealistic cities were successful and continue to this day, including Oneida, N.Y., and Winston-Salem, N.C. But most have either disappeared or remain as museums of antiquity.

After the Revolution and before the Civil War, the only federal involvement in new city development was in the design, layout, and construction of Washington, D.C. in accordance with the brilliant L'Enfant plan. As new states were formed, the planning of their capital cities under state auspices was common practice. Frequently the location of the capitol building was excellent, even though the city design was a dull grid. The most interesting and certainly the most ambitious was Indianapolis, designed by Alexander Ralston, a surveyor for the L'Enfant plan in Washington, for a state-appointed commission.

County involvement in the construction of new communities also has had a long history. Beginning in the early years of coastal settlement, the location of a county courthouse was frequently also the location of a rural county capital. It became the market and political center for what was frequently a substantial area. Courthouse building groups, particularly in Virginia, were frequently the planned nucleus for a new community.

To summarize the 300 years of history of building planned urban centers in the United States prior to the Civil War is to summarize the excitement and idealism of the America that was new and ambitious, inventive, and above all creative. While it is true that in contemporary terms many of the new towns and cities built during the Colonial and pioneering days were seldom based on more than two-dimensional lot and layout plans, they frequently set the pattern for orderly development as these communities grew.

THE ERA OF SPRAWL

In the 100 years since the Civil War, America has grown mainly by unplanned agglomeration. Traces of the plans laid in the earlier era of community building still can be found in some of our cities, but for the most part the beginning traditions of urban design have been buried in random growth.

This growth, in the continuing era of nondesign, has taken place almost entirely in and around pre-existing cities. America was past the time of founding cities; the centers of settlement had been established. True, new municipalities were formed around these centers, but they were mainly artificial boundaries cut into what in this century has become a continuous metropolitan sprawl. Thus a description of new community building from the Civil War to the present can only be a listing of sporadic events, occurring for widely diverse reasons in widely scattered locations.

The first government involvement in new community building in this era, in fact, did not come until World War I. In connection with emergency shipbuilding and armament operations, a series of small but well planned new communities were built with federal financing, the most notable being Yorkship Village south of Camden, N.J. All were sold on the open market after the war and most have virtually disappeared.

During the Depression, the suburban resettlement division of the Federal Resettlement Administration built three notable new towns: Greenbelt, Md., just north of Washington, D.C.; Greenhills, Ohio, north of Cincinnati, and Greendale, Wis., near Milwaukee. While all three of these communities were designed by the best planning talent of the day, they were, in principle, more garden cities than new communities and were not designed to incorporate full employment opportunities within their boundaries.

Simultaneously with these three suburban towns, the federal government was involved in a larger urban settlement experiment which was doomed to failure. The Rural Resettlement Administration attempted to stem rural migration from depressed areas such as Tennessee, Kentucky, Arkansas, and Oklahoma by building a number of scattered villages, most of them under cooperative management. The RRA also attempted to find alternatives for agricultural and mining employment, both of which had achieved the rock bottom of economic viability. For most migrants who had moved to California, the Resettlement Administration also attempted to build new communities as reception centers. Since funds were limited, most of these were small and hardly more than migratory labor camps. The one exception was Yuba City, which survived as a community until it was wiped out by Sacramento River floods in the 1950's.

There is little evidence left anywhere of the rural resettlement attempts, largely because they were too small and were built during a period of depression when economic viability simply was not attainable. With the coming of World War II and the development of new employment centers for workers, the Resettlement Administration disappeared, the Greenbelt communities were disposed of on the open market, and these government ventures were dropped.

Two important federally sponsored new communities were built in association with power and reclamation projects during the 1930's. The first, Boulder City, Nev., was established in 1932 in the desert near the site of the new Boulder Dam, (later Hoover Dam). Boulder City started as a company town, specifically for construction workers, but in 1959 was converted to an incorporated city under Nevada law.

GREENBELT MARYLAND

A Map Prepared by the
Greenbelt Nursery School

● County
▬ Dwellings
PUBLIC BLDGS.

Map No. 5

○ Small Childrens' Playgrounds. (Equipment consists
mainly of a sandbox or climbing apparatus. A few
areas have swings and see-saws or a slide.)

◎ Playgrounds with apparatus for school-age children.

◇ Open areas not designed for play, but used for various
kinds of play, mainly ball of the sand-lot type, by
boys under teen-age.

G Allotment Gardens.

A better example was Norris, Tenn., built by the Tennessee Valley Authority between 1933 and 1935 on a site 21 miles north of Knoxville. It too was constructed originally for employees working on a dam project. Well planned, beautifully located, designed from the start to become a regular incorporated city under the laws of Tennessee, it remains one of the best examples of a new community built under federal sponsorship to be found in the United States. Curiously and unfortunately, it has not served as a prototype for other new community development in the rapidly expanding and successful Tennessee Valley. Not all good planning is contagious.

The final major federal effort in the building of new communities occurred toward the end of World War II as the Atomic Energy Commission found it necessary to isolate its highly secret operations, which required large components of skilled workers. The three atomic energy towns are found in widely scattered areas and some distance from other settlements. The first was Los Alamos, N.M., followed by Oak Ridge, Tenn., and Hanford (Richland), Wash. Of the three, the best designed was Hanford. Both it and Oak Ridge are now operating under their own governments and are economically successful, having developed a reasonably broad base of employment in their areas.

THE PRIVATE ROLE

Of all the trillions of dollars of private investment in urban development in the years 1860-1960, little went into the building of new communities from scratch. The earliest of the few such examples, moreover, were anything but auspicious: the company towns of the 19th century industrial age, which were either built as, or quickly became, slums.

The huge immigration from Europe of unskilled and low-cost workers into the rapidly expanding industrial cities of the Midwest and the North

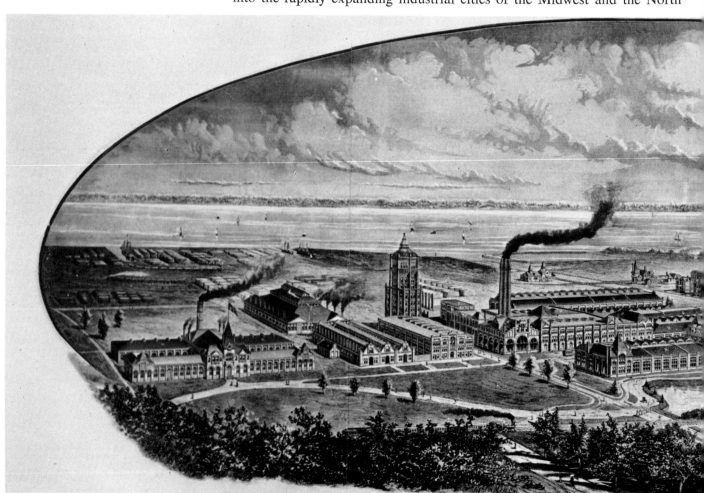

placed a premium on jobs for the immigrants and created a labor surplus situation which placed few demands on the conscience of the employer. Neither federal nor state laws existed providing for decent housing and sanitation, let alone protecting the interests of the workers themselves. Further, because of the frequent isolation of new industrial communities at the minehead or in valley bottoms in Appalachia and elsewhere, industry, which was frequently managed by absentee owners, could conduct its exploitation of its workers from generation to generation with little worry about outside interference. Out of the welter of 19th century company towns from the Atlantic Coast to Lake Michigan, only one stands out as a well planned example of benevolent paternalism applied to the welfare of the workers. This is Pullman, Ill., just south of Chicago, built between 1881 and 1885.

Pullman was well landscaped and designed: Parks, (below) a theater, schools, public library, and other amenities shared its 300-acre site with workers' housing and the Pullman Company plant. It was a rare American example of a completely three-dimensional plan, built with an eye on the over-all appearance of the community and the welfare of its inhabitants. Unfortunately, poor wages and working schedules brought on the great Pullman strike of 1894, which destroyed the harmony of the community.

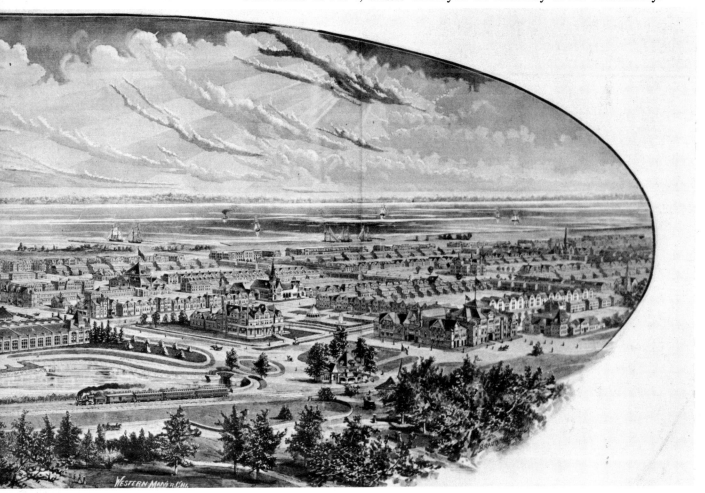

At the turn of the century, industry did begin to build scattered planned company towns for its workers with some design quality. Granite City, Ill., and Vandergriff, Pa., were built just before 1900; Hershey, Pa., was started in 1903, and remains a successful workers' community; Kohler, Wisc., was founded in 1913. Kohler was incorporated as a village from the start; the residents have had full control over governmental affairs, an unusual situation in most company towns.

Two years after the founding of Kohler, work began on Kingsport, Tenn., under the auspices of the Kingsport Development Corp. Kingsport was planned by the then-most-prominent city planner in the United States, John Nolan Sr., with its government-management operations resulting from a special study made on its behalf by the Rockefeller Foundation. Kingsport was not a one-company town. From the beginning it was designed as a multi-industry community and succeeded in drawing to it the first major branch plant of the Eastman Kodak Company, a major publishing house, a major tannery and leather working company, a cement plant, and other industries. The result was that during the Depression Kingsport maintained a high rate of employment and has continued as an important and growing community in eastern Tennessee. Kingsport suffered from inadequate zoning restrictions and has lost much of its original quality, but it remains as the unique example of a privately sponsored, totally new community which has survived through the years as a successful venture.

The influence of the British garden city and new towns movement was felt in many subsequent attempts to establish privately sponsored new communities in various parts of the country. In large part, these attempts were directed towards the development of suburban bedroom communities; they seldom contained the employment component considered today as the essential ingredient of a new community. However, many of these attempts were well designed and made important contributions to the science and art of city planning. The most important of these was, of course, Radburn, N.J., (right), designed by Clarence Stein and Henry Wright as a complete garden city development with shopping centers and industrial location. Radburn was begun in 1928 and unfortunately ran into the financial difficulties of the Depression. It could not be completed. Its design influence, however, has been international: It forms the basis for most contemporary thinking in the separation of pedestrian and automotive traffic, in the development of planned shopping and industrial centers in relation to residential areas, in the provision of greenbelts and adequate park spaces for inhabitants, and in the development of the superblock concept.

The first post-World War II new community was Park Forest, Ill., begun in 1947 by Phillip Klutsnick. Park Forest developers discovered at an early date that public finances would be inadequate to provide public services in the initial stages of development. For the first three years and more, commercial facilities were totally inadequate to satisfy the needs of the new inhabitants and schools were in housing units provided by the developer.

98

America has now entered a new era of urban development. It has some
choices to make. It can let future growth spread out from existing centers in
incoherent and unorganized form—or it can see that growth is planned and
designed in such a way as to create genuine communities that serve the
deepest needs of their inhabitants. It can follow the haphazard practices of
the past 10 decades—or return to the neglected tradition of community
building which, in the nation's first 300 years, created most of the beauty
and amenity that is to be found in America's man-made environment.

BRITAIN'S POSTWAR ACHIEVEMENT

Wyndham Thomas

during World War II, the British central government, readying for postwar rebuilding and population growth, combined with the big cities and surrounding counties to commission comprehensive plans for the major city regions. All of these plans incorporated a new-towns and town-expansion program related to renewal of slum and near-slum city districts at reduced densities.

For example, the Greater London Plan, which covered an area of 2,600 square miles with a population then of over 10 million, deployed a complete four-part strategy. A greenbelt would be defined around the metropolis to prevent its continuing outward spread and to provide recreation areas. New towns and town-expansion schemes would be built beyond the greenbelt to provide homes and work together for a million people from London, thus helping to absorb the pressures which made the greenbelt necessary. Inner London's slum and "twilight" areas would be rapidly rebuilt at lower densities (maximum 200 persons per acre), incorporating better homes, schools, play areas, and parks. And, fourthly, effective means would be found to steer relocating and new industries to the new and expanding towns and to the old industrial regions, the nurseries of Britain's industrial revolution whose basic industries—mining, shipbuilding, and textiles—were (and are) in chronic decline.

These regional plans and associated economic and land-use planning objectives were endorsed and a legislative program produced to secure their fulfillment:

The 1946 Distribution of Industry Act gave the Board of Trade the task of defining as "development areas" those parts of the country overdependent on declining industries and suffering excessive unemployment. To ensure that new industries were steered to these areas, that new factories were not built in already overcrowded city districts, and that (in the conditions of economic crisis of the postwar years) building and plant investment was concentrated on essential (mainly export) industries, the Industrial Development Certificate (IDC) control was introduced. Any firm wanting to build a new factory had first to seek an IDC from the Board of Trade whose decision was based on the criteria outlined. The control has been maintained in successive Acts and extended to offices.

But alongside this stick is a juicy carrot. Firms locating in the "development areas" (by definition, localities with above 3 per cent unemployment) can obtain government grants to cover 25 per cent of building costs, 40 per cent for new manufacturing plant and machinery, £10 ($24) a week for each employee being trained for a new job, and an annual premium worth almost £100 (say $240) for every man on the payroll. The total of these inducements is running at £265 million (say $600 million) a year.

The 1947 Town and Country Planning Act gave firm powers to county councils and larger (above 100,000 population) city councils to plan urban growth, adaptation, and change; and to control development in accordance with their plans. This planning system has been modified several times since then, but the basic structure and aims remain. (The 1947 Act also provided for public recoupment of increases in the development value of land as a result of public investment and planning decisions. This aspect of the Act was discarded in the early 1950's, but a new system for collecting "betterment" has been brought in under the Land Commission Act of 1966.)

The 1946 New Towns Act (re-enacted wth modifications in 1962) gives the Minister of Housing and Local Government power to publish a draft order designating a precise area for development as a new town. The purposes and population of the proposed new town are set out and a public hearing into any objections then held. (Serious difficulties at this stage are anticipated and cleared beforehand by long and detailed discussions with the local authorities principally concerned.) After considering the report of the hearing, the Minister confirms the draft order, but invariably with modification of the proposed area and reassurances over major and minor issues raised.

The Minister then sets up a development corporation to plan and build the new town, but in cooperation with all the public authorities and agencies and private interests necessarily involved. The board of the corporation consists of a chairman, deputy chairman, and up to seven members. All serve part-time and are paid modest salaries—chairman £2,000 ($4,800), members £500 ($1,200). Particular care is taken to appoint people combining a wide range of relevant experience and proved ability, to a degree representative of local authorities and other major interests in the locality.

The board always includes a leading member of the council of the large city (London, Birmingham, Glasgow, etc.) to which the new town is linked.

The board then appoints a full-time chief executive (general manager) and chief officers to serve under him—finance, architecture-planner, estates, engineer, legal, etc. A fully established development corporation will have about 300 full-time staff, excluding labor for outside repair and maintenance work. The board is charged with making and overseeing the implementation of policy. The general manager is responsible for actual policy execution, running the organization, cooperation with all other agencies, financial control, and advising the board on all policy matters.

The Act gives the corporation compulsory purchase (eminent domain) powers over land needed for its purposes. Up to 1959, corporations bought land at "existing-use value." For much the greater part of their acquisitions this meant agricultural value—from say £100 ($240) to £300 ($720) an acre. The rule since 1959 is that they pay the market value of the land for the use to which they propose to put it, less any increase or decrease brought about by the new town as such. In practice this means that the district valuer (a Department of Inland Revenue official) has to assess the likelihood of normal development over a period of 20 years or so in deciding the price (subject to negotiation) which the corporation shall pay. Owners can appeal against his valuation to the independent Lands Tribunal. Up to now, corporations have usually bought about two-thirds of the designated area, leaving in private ownership most of the land not needed for actual development or associated uses.

Before extensive land acquisition, however, the corporation, in consultation with the local authorities and many other interests, prepares and publishes a master plan. The plan shows the broad land-use pattern and highway system proposed and is accompanied by a comprehensive survey report and policy proposals. This is submitted to the Minister who holds a full-scale public hearing before deciding whether to endorse the plan. For implementation the corporation submits detailed planning and financial proposals to the Minister for sectors of the town in accordance with its development program. These too are fully discussed beforehand with the other public agencies involved. The Minister's approval of these detailed proposals constitutes a planning consent and, in effect, an authorization for the advance of the necessary government loans.

All the corporation's costs and investments, including contributions to, for example, agencies responsible for water supply or sewage disposal, are met by 60-year loans from the government at current rates of interest (now 8 per cent). Annual deficiencies are covered by further borrowing until such time as revenues exceed outgoings.

Fourteen new towns were started in the late 1940's, and by the end of 1968 half a million people had gone to live in them. Only one more was started in the 1950's, but since 1962 another 13 have been launched, the latest—and the biggest of them all with a proposed population of 500,000

—being announced in the early days of January, 1969. By the end of the century the combined populations of these 28 new towns will be more than 3 million of an expected total population of 65 to 70 million.

Current central government investment in the new towns by way of 60-year loans to the new-town development corporations is running at the rate of £70 million ($168 million) a year; a sum equal to about 0.2 per cent of the gross national product. By the middle 1970's, investment by the 28 development corporations will reach about £150 million ($360 million) a year. All other agencies—local authorities, public utilities and numerous private concerns—will be investing over £200 million ($480 million) a year.

The 1952 Town Development Act provides government aid to smaller town expansion in the form of 50-per-cent grants for extension of main water supply and sewerage systems. Each scheme is based on a tripartite agreement between the (usually small) town council wanting to expand population and employment, the council of the county in which it lies and which provides the major local government services (education, health and welfare, police, town and country planning, etc.), and a large city (London, Glasgow, Birmingham, Manchester, Liverpool) struggling with housing shortage and overcrowding problems. Because of the tenuous nature of the tripartite agreement, progress under this Act has been much slower than under the New Towns Act. But striking successes are being achieved, especially where the "receiving" town and county councils and the "sending" big-city council set up and finance a joint development board to plan and carry out basic development and attract other public and private investment. Current schemes under the Town Development Act aim at providing about 200,000 homes, of which 50,000 have so far been built, for families from the large cities. Over 20 million square feet of factory space have been built in them to date.

EVOLUTION OF A POLICY

The roots of Britain's new-towns and town-expansion programs go back to Ebenezer Howard. In 1898 he first advocated building clusters of "garden cities" in the rural hinterlands of the vast and still spreading industrial concentrations. The primary aim was—as it still is—to reduce population in the grossly overcrowded, decayed, and densely built inner districts of the great cities. Only by substantial reduction of their populations could these districts be rebuilt to provide much better conditions of life and work for the many millions who would go on living in them. The "garden cities" were to be the means of effecting this "decongestion."

Howard launched two demonstration projects, at Letchworth, 30 miles from London, in 1903, and Welwyn Garden City, 20 miles from London, in 1919. Both depended solely on private capital, with investors accepting a 5-per-cent limitation on dividends. All surpluses above this were to be plowed back "for the benefit of the community." Neither town earned an economic return for several years but both eventually triumphed, wiping out earlier losses and establishing high land and property values. Private enterprise thus showed the way.

Howard and his supporters persistently pressed for a massive publicly backed new-towns program as the essential prerequisite of an even greater program of humane and efficient renewal of the overcrowded working class quarters of London, Glasgow, Birmingham, and the rest. It was their efforts over the years which paved the way for Britain's postwar planning and development programs.

The workings of these programs can best be examined by looking at the ring of early new towns around London. There were eight in all, 20 to 30 miles from central London, started between 1947 and 1950, and initially planned to take 350,000 people. They have achieved this, and their targets have been raised to a total of 550,000 with provision for natural growth beyond. They set out to attract industrial and commercial firms and their staffs from London. Interested firms were offered developed sites which they could lease to build their own premises or, in very many cases, custom-built factories and offices which they then leased. All rents showed a new profit to the corporations, with increases at the agreed review periods. There were no subsidies of any kinds available to these firms.

At the same time, rental homes were offered to any and as many of a firm's staff who were willing to move: usually 60 to 70 per cent. The firm's outstanding employment needs were met by recruitment via the Industrial Selection Scheme. This scheme is administered by the Greater London Council, and seeks to match labor needs in the new and expanding towns with workers in London who have a housing problem and are willing to move out. In addition to relocating firms, quite new enterprises have been established in the new towns, including some American concerns. Recruitment of staffs for them has proceeded in the same way. Specialist, managerial, and professional staffs for the new towns' firms and public services have been recruited on a countrywide basis.

Thus, about 75 per cent of the new families have come from London. About a half of these were either occupying public housing in London or were on the lists kept by the London boroughs of families in housing need because of overcrowding, slum conditions, or redevelopment schemes.

The great majority of the houses in these new towns were built by the development corporations for rent. But over the last 10 years or so, the corporations have increasingly sold land to private builders. The aim now is that in all the new towns about half the new homes shall be built for sale by private firms, the other half being for rent. Up to 1965 housing built for rent attracted a fixed government subsidy of about £30 ($72) a year, but the current subsidy meets the interest charge of about 4 per cent on the capital cost of construction. Each corporation pools these annual subsidies and applies them both to standardize rents for comparable accommodation and to give greater assistance to families in need.

105

New towns, like all new settlements, attract predominantly young married people. But the population of the eight London new towns mirrors very closely the national pattern in terms of income and social groupings. Only the rich and the very poor are underrepresented. The latter group are of particular concern to the public authorities, and special efforts, which are described later, are being made to attract more of them to the new towns. The same applies to retired people, though about 8 per cent of the families in the London new towns are retired people, mostly of very modest incomes who have moved out to live near a married daughter or son.

Most families have settled very quickly into the new towns, and social and mental problems have been minor and transient. There is a high degree of satisfaction with the physical environment, especially in relation to the educational and recreational needs of children. As the corporations, local authorities, and private enterprise have provided the leisure facilities needed, so even the minor grumbles have died away.

Employment has grown with population so that numerically each of the new towns contains sufficient jobs. But a perfect reconciliation is impossible to achieve. The result is that about 80 per cent of those gainfully employed live and work in their town; about 20 per cent go out to neighboring towns and to London, these latter being balanced by an equivalent daily inflow. Manufacturing industry accounts for about 60 per cent of total employment, but (in keeping with trends in all economically advanced countries) the service sector is growing fast. The corporations are now attracting firms in this sector, and especially firms able to offer jobs to the rising number of school-leavers. Unemployment is about 1 per cent.

All but one of these eight new towns achieved a revenue surplus after about ten years and cleared accumulated deficiencies over the next four to seven years. (The eighth new town involved clearing extensive rural slums so that acquisition and reservicing costs were abnormally high.) Four of these towns are substantially completed and have accordingly passed into the ownership of the Commission for the New Towns. (The commission is a central government agency set up to take over completed new towns from their development corporations and to manage their assets until a permanent decision is made about disposal.) The summary of the combined financial results for the four towns is as follows:

New population: 148,000
New houses (public and private): 48,000
Total jobs: 110,000
Net capital advances: £101 million ($242,400,000)
Average rate of interest: 5 per cent
Profit on general revenue: £0.73 million ($1,752,000)
Profit on sales: £0.27 million ($648,000)
Profit on total: £1.0 million ($2,400,000)

This shows a 1-per-cent rate of net profit on the four new towns. But housing accounts for 80 per cent of the total investment, and it is government policy that the housing account be kept in balance, taking one year with another. The net profit of £1 million therefore largely arises from investment in industrial and commercial land and buildings, totalling about £16 million.

THE SECOND ROUND

The new towns program has been expanded substantially in the last six years, after the economic and social successes of the first round had been demonstrated. These later new towns, with ultimate populations ranging from 80,000 to 500,000, will take a sizable share of the larger population growth predicted for the major city-regions; they will provide homes and work together for more families from the still crowded (but less so than 10 years ago) inner-city districts; and they will create economic growth points in carefully selected areas, including in the regions still overdependent on declining industries.

They are to be developed at a much faster rate to meet the rising pressures of population growth and movement. This, and the inclusion of major town expansions involving large-scale urban renewal, predicates a more rapid rate of capital investment to a much higher gross and per capita level.

The major town expansions have been included because, in a closely developed country such as England, it is increasingly difficult to find clear sites for new towns which are not open to some overriding objection. (If California had the same average population density as England its population would be about 150 million!) In addition, on open sites it takes longer to develop an economic base capable of generating a rapid rate of growth. The four towns chosen for expansion have populations of 80,000 to 130,000 and a strong manufacturing industry base as well as established public and private services. These will be exploited to achieve earlier and faster growth than in the open-site new towns.

The development corporations will operate in equal partnership with the existing local authorities, who will continue to exercise in full, but for a rising level of demand and need, their servicing, regulatory, utilitarian, and social functions. The corporations will combine with them in planning and executing the development program for new families and enterprises and in carrying out essential renewal, especially of the city center.

At Peterborough, a cathedral city and industrial center 80 miles due north of London, the population of 80,000 is to be expanded to 170,000 in 15 years. Slower growth will then take it up to 200,000 by the end of the century. It is intended that about half the new families will come from the crowded inner districts of London, and the remainder largely from the rest of London and the southeast of England, where almost a third of Britain's population now lives. Among the 50 per cent or so from inner London, strong emphasis will be placed on attracting unskilled and semi-skilled workers: the lower wage-earners, often with large families, on whom London's housing shortage presses most severely.

107

108

First, existing Peterborough industries will be encouraged to expand, and the development corporation's rental housing program will be geared to meet this expansion. The corporation and the firms, it is intended, will combine to carry out recruitment drives in London in association with the Greater London Council and London Boroughs. Jobs and houses together will be offered—rental housing and also houses for sale, which local builders are ready to provide.

Some local firms already have good training schemes for turning unskilled into semi-skilled workers. Other firms will be encouraged to follow suit, singly or in combination. As part of the recruitment drives, potential newcomers and their families will be brought to Peterborough by bus at the weekends to look over the new houses, the industrial areas and factories, the shopping centers, and the schools. Detailed advice will be given on wage-levels, housing costs, commodity prices, schools, transport, and other services. If necessary—and it probably will be—development corporation staff will be stationed full-time in London to help those families that need it to plan their move, to plan their budgets, and to solve other individual problems.

The second aspect of growth will involve the attraction of firms from London, either to lease or buy serviced sites from the development corporation, or to occupy purpose-built factories or offices. But no subsidies will be available: A return of at least 9 per cent per annum, or its equivalent, will be required.

Private developers and private capital will play a large part in carrying through the total program. Half the new houses will be built for sale, mostly by private firms. Half the investment in sites and buildings for industry and commerce will come from the private sector; and already the air is alive with the rustle of check-books being waved by representatives of a dozen highly respected financial institutions. Private enterprise can operate both in its own interest and in support of public objectives.

Peterborough story is just beginning. The story of some of the first new towns has largely been told. In prospect and in retrospect, Britain's post-war planning and development has been and is immensely worthwhile.

NEW CITIES AND NATIONAL STRATEGY

Some characteristics of America's crowded future are both
predictable and unchangeable: There will be, as we have
seen, as many as 100 million more Americans by the year
2000; they will cause the urbanization of twice the
land area now so classified. Other characteristics are less
predictable, such as the impact and nature of new technolo-
gies, and still others are predictable but eminently sus-
ceptible to change. These last include the waste, the divisive-
ness, the ugliness of present patterns of urban growth.

The instrument of change can be a national urban
growth policy, which enlists all levels of government, and
private individuals and businesses as well, in an effort to
build new patterns that will not have these characteristics.
Such a policy can be installed without doing damage to our
traditions; it can increase, rather than diminish, Americans'
choices of places and environments. And, if backed by a
national commitment to make positive use of the future, it
can work.

That was the conclusion of a cautious, fact-laden report
of the Advisory Commission on Intergovernmental Relations, a body established by Congress and including federal, state, and local officials and legislators. Entitled
"Urban and Rural America: Policies for Future Growth,"
the report did not simply plunge to the conclusion that such
policies were either achievable or desirable. Instead, the
commission painstakingly went through the arguments pro
and con:

Con—*If one policy would be to divert growth from the great cities, it will fly in the face of history. "From ancient Greece to the present, the migration from the countryside to the city has been a source of concern and periodic hand-wringing." Yet it has continued inevitably and inexorably. We lack the knowledge, moreover, to say whether this is good or bad, to weigh the effects of population density, to do a cost-benefit analysis of urbanization. Even if we had the knowledge, attempts to influence the direction of growth would have to involve inducements to people and businesses to locate where they would not normally chose to, which would be an interference with their freedom. And who is to say which communities or regions are to be nourished and which left to die?*

Pro—*Government already influences the direction of growth, but in a haphazard, purposeless way. A national policy would organize these influences and make them explicit. It would also reduce the prospect of government continuing to launch new programs piecemeal as new problems arise. Above all, our cities, our metropolitan areas, and our rural communities all have pressing needs that can only be met with the future in mind.*

"On balance," the commission concluded, "there is a specific need for immediate establishment of a national policy for guiding the location and character of future urbanization, involving federal, state, and local governments in collaboration with the private sector of the national economy." The commission cited, in support of its conclusion, "the diseconomies of scale involved in continuing urban concentration, the locational mismatch of jobs and people, the connection between urban and rural poverty problems, and urban sprawl. In addition to these nationwide effects, such conditions are exacerbating the country's major social and political crisis, i.e., the declining health and vitality of many of our largest cities."

No one has a comprehensive national urban growth policy in his desk drawer fully drafted. But from the commission report and the discussions of the National Committee on Urban Growth Policy (whose recommendations are the final chapter of this book) can be drawn some of its ingredients. They would include:

1. Linkage of economic and physical development. Planning for jobs, for industry, for commerce must be part of the planning of communities. If one of the goals is to provide new choices for low-income people now crowded into urban centers, it does no good to provide housing without jobs, or vice versa; it may do no good to provide both without job-training, counseling, and supportive services.

Economic and community development programs of the federal and state governments are now thoroughly fragmented. They would have to be tightly joined in a single strategy to influence urban growth.

2. The influencing of private decisions. Population movement is the result of millions of individual decisions made for countless complex (and not always rational) motivations. A marginal farm worker is sent the fare north by a relative who has found a messenger's job in the city and is, by comparison, prosperous. A mother, concerned about the education her children are getting, finally convinces her husband that it's worthwhile to make the move to another community with better schools even though they can scarcely afford the least expensive houses there. A manufacturer makes the hard decision that a plant is too far from its markets and sources of materials; the plant is relocated, and a hundred families have the choice of following or losing their jobs.

These kinds of decisions cannot (should not) be compelled by a democratic government, but government can seek to offer additional options. The commission report, for example, proposes federal tax advantages, loans, or direct payments to businesses and industries who locate according to a plan for urbanization. Such incentives might be the additional factor that tips the decision of the manufacturer to stay in an area where jobs are scarce—or, if he is building a new plant, to locate it in an area chosen for planned growth.

Relocation payments to individuals, the commission suggests, could help motivate those who find it hard to pull up stakes and move to places of greater opportunity. The sheer quality of environment that could result from better planned development also could be a magnet to draw both families and businesses to new growth centers.

3. Putting public investments to strategic use. The federal and state governments themselves are major employers. Location of a defense installation, a new university, even a government office complex can mean new economic life for a community, as evidenced by the fact that these decisions often are the subjects of energetic political tugs-of-war in Congress and the state houses. The results of these tugs-of-war often show little resemblance to anyone's idea of rational urbanization planning. If there were an explicit urban growth policy, at least there would be a yardstick to hold these decisions up against. At best, it could lead to strategic location of public employment centers as seeds of economic and population growth.

Government also is a major buyer, and the commission

suggests that it consider preferential treatment of firms who locate according to an urbanization plan. Federal contracts alone add up to more than $85 billion per year. The commission proposes a percentage deduction on both negotiated and competitively bid purchases for goods and services from suppliers located where jobs are needed.

Finally, it is government which lays down the roads, the sewers, and the water lines that make development possible. At present, these investments normally follow, rather than lead, the direction of growth. Many of them are made by local governments, but often with federal or state aid that could be tied to an urbanization policy. Direct federal and state involvement is heavy in building such things as highways, airports, and hospitals, all of which help determine where growth happens.

4. A larger public role in the deployment and development of land. Vacant land is the basic national resource for dealing with growth; urbanization is the filling of land with all of the facilities needed for the people who make up the population projections. The influencing of growth means influencing what happens to vacant land in the places where these people will live. It also means, in some cases, holding land from development as open space or for future use; and preventing the waste of land through development that is haphazard and unplanned.

The commission relates these purposes to the scale at which development occurs. The kind of metropolitan growth which it calls "sprawl"—gradual accretion at the edges of metropolis, house-by-house, building-by-building, street-by-street—can scarcely produce anything but a fragmented end result, particularly with the ineffectiveness of current planning and control devices. The commission suggests that the government aid in the assembly of pieces of land large enough to be planned comprehensively. The basic unit of metropolitan growth then could become the community instead of the single house or subdivision.

These would be among the tools included in an urban growth policy. They would be applied according to an analysis of the kinds of places where Americans live and want to live, from the great cities to small rural counties. The analysis would take into account the problems and growth potential of each, the consequences of allowing some to expand and others to wither, and ways of changing what seem undesirable trends.

The commission offers a model of this kind of analysis in relation to economic activity. It classifies two types of places as "labor surplus areas": rural counties "characterized by an older, underskilled, and undereducated population, re-

sistant to moving"; and inner-city neighborhoods "characterized by considerable underemployment and unemployment, recent out-migration of blue collar industry, and difficulty of resident job seekers in traveling to blue collar jobs in suburbs." Its prescription for application of an urban growth strategy to the rural counties is to provide job training and relocation assistance to the residents, encouraging them to move to places where there are jobs to be found (but not to the cities). For the inner city, it proposes a dual approach of bringing jobs to the residents through attraction of new business and industry; and, at the same time, giving the residents opportunities to move where the jobs are through relocation assistance. (The commission doesn't make it sound all that easy. In this particular analysis, it is dealing specifically with use of incentives to influence the locational decisions of businesses and individuals. Elsewhere it takes due note of the barriers to mobility faced by the poor and minorities.)

What the commission proposes is breaking the deadly interrelationship which these two kinds of problem areas have established, in which the unemployed of the rural counties migrate to become the unemployed of the inner-cities. It is suggesting that alternatives be opened to those who might otherwise follow this tragic migratory pattern, to those already in the cities' growing pockets of despair— and to those American families, not yet formed, who constitute the statistics on future population increase.

These alternatives, the commission says, could be created by channeling growth into four kinds of communities. One consists of the present suburbs, for which the commission suggests changing the nature rather than the already rapid pace of growth by giving more low-income workers a chance to live near expanding suburban employment centers. The second and third would be small rural cities—"urban places" outside of metropolitan areas—and medium-sized cities which are healthy in terms of both their economies and environments and could be expanded into larger centers. The fourth would be entirely new communities, built from scratch with public assistance—and to public standards of population diversity in terms of race and income.

The commission links all of these forms of growth inducement to programs of improvement in the central cities. Indeed, they may be necessary to make central-city improvement possible. Growth itself is not the threat to the cities, at least not to the older cities of the Northeast and Midwest; their growth, in fact, has all but stopped. The threat is, again, in the deadly selectivity of present patterns of growth, in which wealth and leadership move out and large pockets of poverty and social chaos are left behind. The creation of new opportunities for the minorities and the poor to live and work outside of these pockets would allow the cities to renew themselves—for the benefit of those who chose to remain, those who might otherwise be tempted to leave, and those who already have moved to suburbia and might be tempted to return. But these new opportunities must be built before the cities can be rebuilt.

This linkage has been emphasized by one of the nation's foremost renewers of cities, Edward J. Logue, who has a strategy of his own. Logue, president of the New York State Urban Development Corp., proposes that instead of building public housing, government break suburban zoning barriers so that private enterprise could build new developments of 40 to 50 units each which low-income families could rent with subsidies to make up the difference between the market rate and what they can afford. He suggests that, to avoid concentration, the number of such developments in any individual suburb not exceed 5 per cent of its total housing supply.

Logue's companion program would be construction of new communities beyond the fringe of metropolis. With these and the suburban developments providing relocation housing, Logue says, "it becomes possible to demolish a substantial number of structures in the inner city that have outlived their usefulness and replace them with new housing, schools, and other facilities." Here, too, private enterprise would be enlisted to build rent-supplemented housing for low-income families who chose to stay, and there would be a rehabilitation corporation to "stop the deterioration of the existing inner-city housing supply."

Logue's and the commission's strategies mesh in some respects and differ in others. The major points of agreement are (1) that we need a national urbanization strategy, for the sake of present cities as well as future population growth; and (2) that part of the strategy should be construction of entirely new communities. The latter concept long has been advanced by planners and conservationists. Now, for some decidedly pragmatic reasons, it may be an idea whose time has come.

If any idea can be said to have a single parent, that of "new towns" was fathered by Ebenezer Howard, an English court reporter and sometimes inventor, in a slim, turn-of-the-century book entitled "Garden Cities of Tomorrow." Howard was no anti-urbanist: In the book he painstakingly classified the virtues as well as the faults of town and countryside. His ideal Garden City was an attempt to combine the virtues of both and eliminate the faults. The construction of Garden Cities, moreover, was to be tied in the long term to renewal of London and other great urban centers.

The book attracted considerable interest; Howard became a popular lecturer, founded the Garden City Association, and saw two examples, Letchworth and Welwyn, built in his lifetime. It was only with the need for post-World War II reconstruction, however, that his idea, kept alive by loyal followers, found its way into the national planning policies of Britain and other European countries. New towns incorporating many of Howard's concepts, particularly in respect to the relationship between buildings and landscape, became an accepted part of postwar European efforts to cope with urbanizations.

American new towns share the same roots, but are largely a phenomenon of the 1960's. By count of the Department of Housing and Urban Development, 64 new communities have been completed or substantially begun here in postwar years and nearly 40 of them in this decade. The department's definition of a new community includes a degree of economic self-sufficiency and a land area of 1,000 acres or more. The current generation of American new towns range in size from 1,200 to 53,800 acres and in eventual population from 4,000 to 270,000. They are located in 18 states, but half are in California, Arizona, and Florida, with their benign climates and recreational advantages. Four-fifths are within metropolitan areas, and so-called "retirement communities" account for a sizable portion of the more remote one-fifth.

All are private ventures. The building of new towns in America—and therefore decisions as to their nature and location—has been left to private developers and corporations. The government offers two forms of assistance: federal guarantees of mortgages up to $25 million on land for new communities, and of up to $50 million on debentures issued by developers to meet the large "front-end" costs of land and community facilities. The mortgage guarantees were enacted into law in 1965, but none has yet been issued; a major reason is that the amortization period is 10 years, far less than the time it takes to make a new town a going enterprise. The debenture guarantees were part of the Housing Act of 1968 and by early 1969 had attracted nearly 20 serious applicants. Guarantees are limited to a total of $250 million at any one time, however.

The impact of new towns on the face of America, in fact, can only be limited so long as they remain an industry rather than an instrument of public policy. They are and *will be, in the first place, few in number, serving only a tiny fraction of total population growth. A new town is a "patient" investment, requiring large outlays long before returns begin; it is thus a noncompetitive investment in a tight money market. Land in town-size amounts is hard to find and assemble without public powers of eminent domain. Privately developed new towns, moreover, by definition must serve the market, which tends to fill them with housing for middle- to upper-income families rather than the poor. Some—notably Columbia, Maryland, and Reston, Virginia—plan lower-income housing, but that is thanks to the individual developers' social consciences. The federal debenture guarantees require only that an unspecified amount of low-income housing be "encouraged" in the towns assisted.*

Making new communities part of a national urban growth strategy requires stronger public incentives to see that they are built where and how they will be needed. Private enterprise can—and should—be heavily involved in the building process, but public policy should influence decisions about location of new communities—and require that they accommodate a significant share of the poor and minorities whose main recourse now is the inner-city. New communities also need to be larger in size and numbers to make a noticable difference in the way growth occurs. They need to be new cities, with the scale and diversity that implies, rather than new towns. This means public investment—money that can be returned (with profit) and reused, as Britain's experience shows, but enough money to get the city-building process started.

Something other than money also is needed, both for a new cities program and for the urbanization policy of which it must be part. The present mechanisms of government are inadequate to devise such a policy and carry it out—to stimulate the building of new cities, to organize the growth that will occur on the edges of metropolis, to rebuild our present urban centers, to create others by expansion of small communities. These mechanisms must be structured before the building process can begin. Designs for doing so are offered in the following three chapters.

Britain has built a high degree of amenity and liveliness into its postwar new towns (this page). Berlin, landlocked, is building two new towns within the city limits. Markisches Viertel (right) will have a population of some 50,000.

THE NEED FOR NEW MECHANISMS

William L. Slayton

there is no dearth of sound, well-considered ideas for ways in which the pattern of urban growth should be changed. There is a dearth of mechanisms for carrying these ideas out. If we want to change the pattern, we must create these mechanisms within the institutions of government at all levels, including some crucial levels at which government institutions are now, for all practical purposes, simply nonexistent.

Let me expand on this point by attempting to sort out what the various levels of government in our federal system are now doing about growth, what they might do, and what kind of mechanisms they would need. First, the federal government itself has a variety of grant programs to aid growing communities in building hospitals, libraries, sewer and water systems, roads, airports, and other facilities. It stimulates housing development through mortgage guarantees and direct subsidies, which in recent years have been increasingly aimed at the needs of lower-income families. It encourages planning by requiring comprehensive plans as a condition of some grant programs, and by helping to pay for the drafting of the plans. Recently it has offered mortgage and "front end" loan guarantees to developers of entire new communities. And finally, of course, the federal government *causes* growth to occur around its own installations. The decision to put a military base or atomic energy facility in a given location is, ipso facto, a decision about where growth will happen.

There are two problems with all of this federal activity. The first is that it is inadequate to the scale of growth as it is occurring. In the fiscal 1969 federal budget, housing and community development programs add up to $2.3 billion, which is 1.3 per cent of total budget expenditures. To put this figure in further perspective, in the same fiscal year the government will spend $4.2 billion for highways alone. National investment in the direction of growth is a matter of low priority.

The second problem is that these programs are spread throughout the agencies of the federal government and not tied together by any noticeable sense of strategy. The federal effort has much in common with the present pattern of growth, in that both are fragmented, unorganized, and piecemeal. Even when the federal government induces growth through construction of a major employment center, it does so with little thought to the developmental consequences. A recent example was the decision to locate a $300 million Atomic Energy Commission accelerator in tiny Weston, DuPage County, Illinois. AEC had a lengthy list of criteria for selection of the site, but they had little to do with urbanization planning. The Department of Housing and Urban Development was not consulted. The accelerator will increase by 50,000 or more the population of DuPage County which, at the time of its selection, had neither a professional planner or a planning commission.

After-the-fact efforts are being made to deal with the consequences, but the point is not what happens to DuPage County. The point is that the federal government wasted a major opportunity to plant the seeds of growth with purpose, and thus to influence the shape of urbanization. Similar waste has marked the $50-billion-plus interstate highway program, which has until recently been planned with mainly vehicular needs in mind. Transportation is perhaps the most powerful determinant of urban form, the most permanent of frameworks for development. Yet, by and large, the impact of the interstate highway program on the face of America will be inadvertent and unplanned.

At the federal level, then, there is need to make growth a subject of higher priority and conscious national policy—and for mechanisms to carry this policy through. As long as programs which influence growth are everybody's business, lodged in a variety of departmental nooks and crannies, their coherent strategic use will continue to be nobody's business. There must be, at the highest level of the Executive branch, someone, some mechanism, to pull the strands together into a fabric of conscious design. It could be the newly created Urban Affairs Council, if it turns out to have sufficient power; it could be the office of the Vice President, if that office could give the subject the attention it requires; it could be a super-Secretary of domestic affairs somewhat more equal than his fellow members of the Cabinet.

This person, or this office, would have the responsibility for drafting an urban growth policy, for applying it to the day-to-day decisions of government, and for reporting annually, to or through the President, on the direction of the nation's development. The specifics of the task would include:

1. Organizing individual federal assistance programs for greater coordinated effect and with a sense of their future consequences as well as immediate impact.

2. Developing new federal tools to influence the deployment of land and

population, including incentives to businesses and individuals to make locational choices that contribute to desirable directions of growth.

3. Holding federal investment decisions—on highways and public works, on major installations—up against a national growth policy, so that each dollar yields not just mileage or square footage but a better future environment.

4. Applying conditions to federal aids to state and local governments so that they advance the policy's aims.

This is a prescription, not just for spending more, but for spending better. Right now we are underutilizing billions of federal dollars by disregarding their potential impact on the pattern of the nation's development. Grant-in-aid programs have their own individual objectives and are tied in webs of tiny administrative strings that frustrate their state and local users. They should be brought together to serve larger objectives, relating to the shape of the nation's future, and should carry fewer but larger strings.

ENTER THE STATES

To put it another way, the national government should apply a firm policy framework which seeks to influence where growth occurs and to assure that federally aided development serves the needs of all, in particular the poor and minorities. But within that framework, state and local governments should have maximum flexibility in how they go about the task. Experimentation should be encouraged: There is no single ideal design for the environment, no ideal city that would be as well suited to the valleys of California as to the meadows of New Jersey.

The states are particularly well suited to play a positive, creative role in shaping urban growth. In our federal system, the states are given crucial powers over both development and local government. The cities and counties are their creatures. The zoning and other regulatory powers exercised by local governments are delegated from the states. And the states, like the federal government, heavily influence the location of population and economic activity through investments in highways, universities, and other facilities.

The difficulty has been that the states, even more than the federal government, have largely failed to use these powers and investments in terms of achieving more rational patterns of urban growth. To put it bluntly, they have been notoriously neglectful of the problems that urbanization has brought. Many of the statehouses have remained bastions of rural interests, narrowly defined, long past the time when their populations have shifted to urban areas. Reapportionment is beginning to redress this anachronism, but with the shifts of population within metropolitan areas, much of the change in representation has been from the farms to the suburbs. This kind of change does not automatically guarantee increased sensitivity to the danger in present patterns of urban growth.

Nevertheless, there has been such an increase in many of our more progressive states, a new awareness that this danger is a threat to the continued health and stability of its rural as well as urban areas—and that somehow new patterns must be found. Seventeen states have established major agencies to deal with urban problems, most in the past few years. Some have begun to take a direct hand in urban growth: New Jersey has established the Hackensack Meadowlands Development Commission to turn 18,000 strategically located acres a half hour from Manhattan into a new community for as many as a half million people. The commission has authority to see that localities holding part of the land make development decisions according to its master plan. Of even larger scope, the New York State Urban Development Corp. was established in 1968 with broad powers—and authority to borrow up to a billion dollars. The corporation can acquire land, dispose of it for planned development, or itself undertake projects ranging from low-income housing to entire new communities.

An agency of this kind could be the key mechanism in a new federal-state partnership to take a positive hand in urban growth. Within the framework of a national growth policy, the state would establish its own more detailed urbanization plan, determining what land should remain in agricultural production, what should be retained as open space, and what should be used for future development. A state-chartered development agency or corporation—either wholly public or a quasi-public body including both public and private interests—would implement the plan. Through federal loans or grants, it would acquire the land to be reserved for open space and the land to be developed well in advance of need (or, alternatively, leave the land in its owners' hands and acquire easements or development rights determining its future use).

The state-chartered agency, whose jurisdiction could be statewide, local, or metropolitan, would phase development according to the pace of growth. When the time came for a given area to be put to use, the agency would make a fine-grain development plan, install the necessary public facilities, reserve some plots for such public uses as parks and school sites, and sell or lease parcels for private construction of housing, shopping, and industry. The area need not be vast and remote, and the development need not be an entirely new community: The process could apply as well to leftover land within metropolis or even surplus public lands within cities.

What I am proposing may seem an expensive and authoritarian scheme. In reality, however, it is not expensive; it can be self-supporting. On a long-term basis, money from the sale and lease of land could finance the acquisition program, the public improvements, and the planning process, as it has in Britain and other nations where similar approaches have been utilized. The money for public facilities has to be spent anyway, whether growth takes haphazard or planned form. As for authoritarianism, it does represent a departure from the laissez-faire approach to land development, which is the only approach that we, in this century, have known. The justification, of course, is that we have a stake in the disposition of the nation's resources, including open land, and in the quality of environment which we and our children will inhabit. The choice of asserting the public's stake may be a hard one, politically and otherwise, but it may be the only choice adequate to cope with impending growth.

BACK IN METROPOLIS...

Most of this growth, in the meantime, will occur on the fringes of present metropolitan areas. Here too the state can play a key role, one that involves the levels of government which, in our present structure, do not yet exist. Those who are already prepared to brand me a subversive surely will have a prediction of what I will say next: that the answer to metropolitan problems is metropolitan government, wiping out all of the present, paralyzing boundaries of local jurisdictions.

If this is the only answer—and I am sure it is not—we will have to live with metropolitan problems for generations to come. Local jurisdictional boundaries are not prepared to fall before an assault of logic. They will be defended to the death, particularly in the well-heeled, increasingly populous, increasingly powerful suburbs. Moreover, there are good reasons to question whether these jurisdictions should be wiped out, even if that were a political possibility. We are in an era when Americans—particularly, but not only, the young and the minorities—are reaching out to touch their institutions of government, are asking that these institutions be more responsive, that they give individual citizens more sense of controlling their own destinies. It defies logic to have the residents of a 20,000-population suburb enjoy self-government while 20,000 blacks in a vast urban ghetto are all but unrepresented. But it also seems inconsistent to talk about eliminating small jurisdictions at a time when urban government is being asked to decentralize.

The answer may lie in sorting out those functions that are local, leaving them to local jurisdictions; and those functions that shape the development of the metropolitan area, creating a new metropolitan governmental entity to handle them. Examples of local concerns are schools, libraries, recreation, social services, police and fire protection. Examples of metropolitan functions that shape development are transportation, air and water resources, conservation of open space, major land use planning, major utilities, and waterways.

None of the latter can be adequately handled by local governments acting alone. Some are in the hands of special districts and authorities of metropolitan scale, but the very existence of these single-purpose bodies works against comprehensive metropolitan planning and development. Most, moreover, are free of political accountability. What is needed is a multi-purpose metropolitan agency to handle metropolitan development problems, elected either by the citizens of metropolis or by their local elected officials. Local jurisdictions would remain intact to handle local problems.

We could call this larger agency a metropolitan council, borrowing the name as well as a partial precedent from the councils of governments

(COGs) which have proliferated in recent years. The growth of the COGs was spurred by their eligibility for federal metropolitan planning grants. Composed of local elected officials, their strength is in encouraging joint consideration of plans and problems, their weakness in the inability to make binding decisions. The metropolitan council would have the power to make a majority decision stick.

The metropolitan council also could be the agency to carry out the kind of large-scale development described earlier (and in the next chapter). One of its concerns—surely the most controversial—should be housing. Local jurisdictions cannot continue to have the right to limit the housing choices available to the poor and minorities in metropolis. The states, which would be the creators of the metropolitan councils, would cede them the power to override exclusionary zoning and other regulations. The state also would set the boundaries of metropolitan areas, and thus the jurisdictions of the councils. (One option would be to make the boundaries of the county contiguous with those of metropolis and give the county government the powers proposed for the metropolitan council.)

If this sounds visionary, expansionist, that is the nature of growth. Growth means expansion and it requires vision. Many of our current frustrations result from the failure of our institutions to grow with population, to expand in competence and jurisdiction along with the problems—and the opportunities—that growth brings. It is past time to bring them in scale with the future.

SOME PROBLEMS OF METROPOLIS, *including the pollution of the air, are common to cities and suburbs alike. The danger is that metropolis, for the most part, has developed no effective means of dealing with these shared problems.*

Smog is no respecter of city limits, nor is the pollution of water. Yet most problem-solving powers are held tightly within jurisdictional boundaries. When special districts are created on a metropolitan-wide basis, they usually deal with just one problem without relation to others.

The automobile helps smudge the air, but causes other forms of pollution as well. Freeways and parking lots dominate downtown Houston, blighting land and cityscape.

Within the city, pedestrians and public transportation are caught in the tangle of the streets. Sorting them out from automobiles and trucks, using fewer vehicles to transport more people in metropolis, have been matters of low priority. The tangle is the so-far accepted price of the independence and individuality of the private car

Unplanned, undirected, largely uncontrolled, the development of metropolis steadily lays waste resources, upsets the balance of man and nature.

It is hard to believe, but it has taken continuing citizen pressure to stay the gradual filling in of San Francisco Bay.

THE ORGANIZATION OF GROWTH

Henry Bain

every few months, metropolitan America will be building all the houses, shopping centers, schools, industries, sewers, and other things needed to create entire cities. The challenge is to organize this urban development so as to build new communities that are physically coherent, economically sound, and socially stable, instead of permitting it to be scattered in bits and pieces over many square miles.

In order to create better-organized urban communities, there must be better organization of the process by which urban development occurs. In any urbanizing area, decisions as to what shall be built, when, and where are made by a large number of individuals and organizations, including home builders, shopping center developers, industrial corporations, institutions, sanitary authorities, school boards, state highway departments, and many others. We cannot depend upon some "invisible hand" to guide their activities toward the creation of the kind of community that we desire. There must be some kind of an organizational entity to take initiative, to make plans, and to encourage, coordinate, and schedule the multifarious public and private actions that produce a viable community.

In the rare cases where a single landowner possesses a tract large enough for the development of a new community, the private developer may play this role, working in cooperation with the local and state governments. But few large and well-located tracts remain in our metropolitan areas, and the odds against the successful assembly of such a tract are very high, even for an unusually well-financed developer. Therefore, responsibility for organizing the development process will ordinarily have to be vested in government.

In the outlying parts of the typical metropolitan area, however, responsibility for the functions relating to urban development is divided among a large number of governmental units. The governmental fragmentation is both functional and geographical. Functions are usually divided among many kinds of units, such as county, township, school district, and sanitary authority.

If an attempt were made to end this fragmentation by concentrating responsibility in a single unit, we would probably find that no existing local government has the ability to do government's part of the urban development job. These local units are ordinarily rural or small-town governments that lack the legal powers, financial resources, staff capabilities, and leadership sophistication needed to superintend the construction of a coherent environment. They were established at various times, mostly in the distant past, to perform a gradually lengthening list of specialized functions (administration of justice, care of the poor, education, public health, etc.) and to build the associated public facilities. The task of putting together all of these facilities in a package with a much larger amount of private construction, in the form of a new or expanded community, is a quite different proposition that requires a different kind of governmental instrumentality.

The purpose of this paper is to suggest such an instrumentality, one that would be capable of organizing growth on the metropolitan fringes so that the end result is the creation of strong and distinct communities, rather than haphazard sprawl. It would be called an urban development district. Such a district would be created under authority of the state, and would encompass both open land and some existing localities. The task of the district would be to plan and bring into being new development within its boundaries. The normal operating functions would remain lodged in the existing local governments. For a stated period, however, all of their development functions would devolve to the district. At the end of this period, when the planned development was substantially completed, the district would be dissolved. Operation and maintenance functions would be assumed by the local governments or turned over to a new governmental unit whose boundaries matched that of the district. The result in the first instance would be a cluster of expanded communities, in the second a new community.

While the district would be created by the state, it could be administered by either the state, a county, or, if the land had been recently annexed by a city, a municipal government. Similarly, the planning and execution of the new development could be in the hands of an agency created by any of these levels of government. The agency would have to be staffed with a wide range of skills, however: Its concerns would go beyond physical development to the economic base of the district and the social environment of the new community, or expanded communities, that would result from its activities.

Still another organizational possibility would be the establishment of a public-private corporation, in which control is shared by government and private investors. This might be an ideal means of enlisting the capital and talents of a large corporation in the task of community-building. Many of the urban development functions ordinarily performed by government might be delegated to such an entity, subject to limitations designed to safeguard the public interest. However, there would still be a need for an organizational enity within the state or local government, to negotiate the terms on which functions are to be delegated and to perform any functions that cannot be delegated to private interests.

THE AGENCY'S FUNCTIONS

Whatever its organizational form, the agency would perform within the urban development district several functions which are essential to the creation of communities, and which are usually performed imperfectly and incompletely if at all.

First of all, the agency would perform some of the functions of *entrepreneurship*. Whether it is a public-private corporation or a strictly public entity, the agency should play the role that would be expected of the private developer of a new community if all of the land were in a single ownership. Entrepreneurship includes taking initiative to call forth the many public and private activities needed to create new or expanded communities, coordinating these in time and space, providing the drive to overcome obstacles and the follow-up to keep every phase of the process moving along on schedule, assuming responsibility for the whole undertaking so that no necessary element is overlooked or neglected, and performing or securing the performance of any functions that would otherwise be lacking.

A second essential function of the agency would be to apply methods for *securing private development* in order to assure timely completion. Heretofore, government has confined itself largely to the regulation of private development by zoning ordinances which limit the uses to which land may be put, the size of buildings, and their placement on lots. As urbanization proceeds, land is rezoned for more intensive development upon petition by individual owners. This kind of regulation, essentially passive and negative, cannot produce an imaginative kind of urban design, making efficient use of the land, preserving natural beauty, and blending a variety of structures in a coherent three-dimensional design; nor can it assure that development will proceed in an orderly manner, bringing each part to completion at the right time.

The agency would employ new and improved zoning techniques to stimulate and guide development of areas designated for low and medium densities. Owners of sizable tracts would be encouraged to apply for planned-unit zoning, which enables developers to produce better-designed residential communities with a mixture of housing types and neighborhood shopping facilities, subject to public control over general layout, density, and schedule. Most other land in the district would be rezoned on the initiative of the agency, rather than on a piecemeal basis at the request of individual owners.

Land designated for intensive development, such as a town center, high-rise apartments, and industrial parks, would be acquired by the agency for resale or lease to private developers, subject to the condition that construction proceed promptly in accordance with plans prepared by the agency. This technique, already familiar in urban redevelopment, is needed to assure the satisfactory completion of these intensive developments, often involving mixtures of complementary activities in multi-level designs, which are too complex to be achieved by regulating the activities of numerous landowners through zoning.

The agency also would acquire and dispose of any lower-density land whose owners are unwilling or unable to develop it in accordance with the district's plans and schedule.

Another function of the agency would be to prepare and execute a coordinated and synchronized public improvements program, in order to assure that all community facilities—roads, water and sewerage, schools, community centers, libraries, playgrounds, etc.—are provided in an economical manner and are available when needed. At present, public improvements for a newly developing area are ordinarily provided by many public agencies with limited cooperation in planning and scheduling. By coordinating the design of these facilities and synchronizing their construction, it is possible to reduce construction costs and increase the efficiency of related facilities. Equally important, this technique can encourage and guide private development in desired directions by making available the full complement of public facilities from areas that are not ready for development.

The agency would formulate a public improvements program for the district in cooperation with all of the public agencies concerned (local school board, regional sanitary authority, state highway department, etc.), and would coordinate the execution of the program. While the agency would take over the responsibilities for development within the district that were formerly exercised by other public agencies, these agencies would retain their operating responsibilities in the district (unless a new community government is established). Each public agency would have a voice in the design of the facilities which it will operate, but the urban development agency would have the last word in case of conflict among the specialized agencies.

Finally, the agency would provide the capital needed to finance the entire package of community facilities, in time to assure the availability of these facilities when they are needed. One of the greatest defects of the present development process is the lack of capital to finance the facilities needed by the new population. Many suburban governments lack the assessable base or the statutory authority needed to borrow the sums required for schools, roads, and other facilities. As a result, the suburban population may go for years without all of the facilities required by a well-rounded community.

The state, county, or city government that establishes the agency would provide it with sufficient capital to finance land acquisition and public improvements for the district. It would repay this capital from money paid

by operating agencies (or a permanent new-community government) at the time they take over public facilities upon completion. The permanent agencies, in turn, would recover the cost of the facilities by taxes, special assessments, and user charges levied on residents and properties in the urban development district in the ensuing years. The agency would also have profits from the sale or lease of land designated for intensive development, which it could use in repaying capital and interest and covering its other expenses.

THE DEVELOPMENT PROCESS

The most direct way to describe how these functions would be performed is to follow through the process of creating a new community, step-by-step. This would be the sequence:

1. *Designate the urban development district.* This would be a function of the state, or of a county or city government acting under state enabling legislation. The district would be located where local or regional plans call for a sizable amount of urban development in the near future—perhaps along a new freeway extending outward from the central city, or in a watershed that is about to be sewered.

All remaining steps would be taken by the agency, subject to policy direction by the state or local government and subject to specific approval of development plans.

2. *Temporarily prohibit development within the district.* This would be necessary in order to prevent accelerated development in anticipation of the new public facilities that will be provided for the new community. Exceptions could be made to permit building on individual lots within subdivisions that are already substantially developed. Landowners who do not wish to hold their land temporarily idle would be given an opportunity to sell it to the agency at the current value.

3. *Ascertain the value of all land in the district as of the date immediately preceding its designation.* This would be necessary to establish a fair price to be paid for land that the agency will acquire, without inflation of the price by the announcement of plans for a new community.

4. *Prepare a general development plan for the district.* The plan would be prepared by the agency in consultation with all public agencies concerned (county school board, regional sanitary authority, state highway department, etc.), with citizens of the entire metropolitan area, and with residents and landowners of the tract. The plan would be subject to approval by the governor in the case of a state agency, or by the local legislative body in the case of a county or city agency.

5. *Prepare detailed plans and designs for each part of the district.* These would be prepared on a staged basis, so experience gained in the planning and development of the first parts of the new community could be applied in

the later parts. These plans and designs would likewise be subject to approval by the governor or local legislative body.

6. *Prepare a program of private development.* This would state the kinds, amounts, and costs of private development called for by the development plan. It would be prepared concurrently with the detailed plans and designs, and with them would serve as a basis for informing landowners and prospective developers about opportunities in the district. It would also be used in promotional activities among potential commercial and industrial occupants.

7. *Prepare a program of public improvements.* This would state the kinds, amounts, and costs of public improvements called for by the development plan. It would be prepared concurrently with the detailed plans and designs, and with them would serve as a basis for reaching agreement among all public agencies as to the public improvements to be provided in the district.

8. *Prepare a schedule of development.* The schedule would specify the time at which each public improvement and each portion of private development should be started and completed. It would be prepared by the agency, acting in cooperation with the various public agencies and with major landowners and developers, and would be subject to approval by the governor or local legislative body.

9. *Construct public improvements.* The improvements might be built by the cognizant public agencies (such as the county public works department or the school district) or by the agency.

10. *Undertake private development.* Single-family housing and some small-scale apartment and commercial construction would be provided by private enterprise operating in accordance with zoning regulations and subdivision controls. The agency would secure more intensive development by acquiring land and selling or leasing it to developers or to large commercial or industrial occupants, subject to agreement as to the character and timing of development. The agency would also acquire and re-sell land designated for lower densities if it will not otherwise be developed in accordance with the schedule.

11. *Administer the development process.* This would be a continuing and complex job, from the time the agency first provides for public improvements and private development until all construction is completed. The agency would be responsible for keeping all participants in the development process informed, resolving conflicts between organizations, expediting activities which fall behind schedule, assuring that all agreements are adhered to, and performing any necessary development functions that would otherwise be neglected.

During the later stages of development, the agency would gradually be superseded by the regular units of local government (or by a new and permanent governmental unit for the new community) until the district is finally dissolved.

12. *Provide for public services.* From the time that development begins, there would be a need for a steadily growing array of services—police and fire protection, traffic control, recreation, education, etc. Each of these would be provided as a matter of course by the various departments of local government, but the agency should be prepared to make temporary arrangements for services in cases where the responsible agency is not able to keep pace with development.

By the time development is nearing completion, the appropriate agencies (or new-community government) should have accepted responsibility for all of the public facilities.

13. *Dissolve the development district.* When development is substantially completed, the urban development district would be dissolved. The completion of any remaining development called for by the plan, and any new development or redevelopment that might subsequently be desired, would be entrusted to private enterprise and the appropriate public agencies, working within the framework of adopted plans, zoning, and all agreements governing land use and development. The new community would continue to be treated as a separate entity for purposes of financing public improvements and recapturing the initial investment of capital. The development agency would no longer have responsibility for the new community, but would continue to perform its functions in other urban development districts.

The urban development district, as proposed above, may appear to be beyond the realm of the politically possible. Surely there is little or no precedent in this country for wiping out the existing structure of local government and installing a new kind of governmental instrumentality, even on a temporary basis.

But none of the other features of this proposal is without a strong precedent. Qualities of entrepreneurship can be found in state and local governments, especially in the promotion of industry and tourism, and in urban renewal. Planned-unit zoning is gaining wide acceptance, and blanket rezoning on the initiative of the responsible public body has always been contemplated by zoning law. Public acquisition of land for disposal to private developers is standard practice in urban renewal, and in the industrial development activities which undertaken by many local governments already are in a more or less systematic manner. And a local government with sufficient borrowing power to raise the capital needed to finance new public facilities for a growing urban population is by no means a rarity.

While each of these components of the idea has ample precedent, it would be very difficult to find a local government, anywhere in the United States, which is effectively employing all of these techniques in a concerted fashion, with respect to all governmental functions that affect development, in an area that is undergoing urbanization.

Thus the challenge turns out, as at the beginning, to be fundamentally a matter of organization—creating a competent governmental instrumentality and combining in it all of the powers needed to shape the inevitable urban growth into a new community. The urban development district is proposed as a recognition of the fact that urban development, or community-building, is a distinct governmental function, requiring a governmental unit with distinctive qualifications.

THE NEW TOWNS MOVEMENT launched by Ebenezer Howard had its first realization in two English communities of which one was Welwyn, built in 1919. Welwyn, with its winding streets, axial parks, and close relationship to nature, is Howard's "Garden City" in classic form.

More than 85 per cent of Welwyn's residents work in the town. The character of its dwellings has remained consistently pleasant through several generations of construction.

Quite another approach to new-town planning is represented in Cumbernauld, near Glasgow. All facilities of the town center are gathered in a great concrete ship of a building straddling the main highway. The housing is ringed around it, beyond a moat of land.

The dwellings of Cumbernauld are varied (and not always distinguished) in design. Perhaps the most successful element of its plan are the handsomely landscaped paths which wind through the buildings and under the roads, frequently widening into a small plaza or playspace.

The town of Tapiola, near Helsinki, is the favorite European stop of architectural pilgrims: Every element of the town shows painstaking design. Tapiola was built, not by government, but by a private nonprofit organization.

A tall office building marks the center of Tapiola, shown here at Christmastime. Apartment buildings and factories all are surrounded by the forest, left nearly undisturbed on the site.

America's Tapiola is Reston, Virginia, whose first village is ringed around a man-made lake (the village center is the horseshoe shape left of the tall apartment tower). Reston also respects the land, also was privately developed, and shows a high standard of design. The attention paid architecture and amenities, however, had its price: Reston's "front-end" costs were high and caused it financial difficulties.

Taking the main path from the parking lot to Reston's first village center, residents enter a pedestrial preserve. Cars are nowhere present in the center; are, in fact, all but out of sight behind the buildings.

The other close domestic equivalent to a European new town is Columbia, Maryland, another private venture. Columbia is being developed outward from the town center, whose beginnings are seen here through a fountain, in a series of villages which are, in turn, clusters of neighborhoods. All are linked by pedestrian ways and a minibus system.

The most notable aspect of Columbia's development has been the process by which it was planned. The physical layout followed analysis of what community facilities each nucleus—town, village, and neighborhood center—should provide. The village center shown left, for example, has an enclosed swimming pool, a community meeting hall, a small library, and, in construction, a secondary school, all grouped around its shopping square.

A FRESH START

William E. Finley

If we are to accommodate America's urban growth in this last generation of the century, we must have a three-pronged attack. First, we must allow existing cities to rebuild and reorganize, sustaining and enhancing their values, and making them livable for centuries to come. Second, we must rationalize suburban growth through community design. Third, we must build new cities, not new towns, beyond commuting distance of existing cities. They can be located in the open countryside, on virgin lands, or they can grow up around existing small towns.

I am purposely referring to new cities, not new towns.

If we allocate one-half of the coming 100 million people to existing peripheral growth around existing cities and 10 per cent to small towns and farms, the remaining 40 million would require the building of 20 cities of one million people each and 200 new towns of 100,000 each.

The locational planning, financing, and construction of new cities is a task which our society can handle. We have most of the management tools and an understanding of the economics. Ideas about social programs and financial resources are available. We lack only the public policy framework within which these tools can be put to work.

The location of cities, for instance, is a far less difficult problem for us than it was for our forefathers who had to look for large bodies of water for shipping and for main-line train terminals. Today's general mobility, innovations in utilities, road-building freedom, air movement, and decreasing importance of agriculture all make it easier to locate sites. While one cannot ignore the basic telephone, airport, highway, and rail networks of the country, they are much less a straight jacket than previous city-locating criteria. New criteria can and should be used: spacing between cities, climate, natural terrain, access to wilderness, or the existence of small- or medium-size towns with sufficient leadership to assist in building for expansion.

New cities offer unusual opportunities for innovation in democratic institutions, in public-private cooperation, in municipal organization. (The prevention of overlapping jurisdictions might be one happy by-product.) They also offer a chance to devise new systems for convenience, safety, easy movement, and esthetic enjoyment. Perhaps most important of all, they provide the psychological benefits of a fresh start.

Obsolete practices such as standard zoning, parking on the street, school-bussing, on-street loading, and highway clutter can all be planned out of a new city. Even in the case of less tractable problems such as land speculation, water waste, inadequate transit, crowded housing, and unsafe streets, every conceivable precaution can be taken to keep them from occurring in a new city.

Both national parties have expressed the belief that new cities will assist in opening new choices for the population of the ghettos. A responsible, sensitive relocation program with tools such as subsidized housing, job training, family counseling, nursery schools, and other aids could build fresh opportunities for families trapped in the inner city. The same tools could be used to prevent reghettoization.

There is a sound economic rationale for new-city building as well. Assuming the ability to buy land, we have learned that the economics of urbanization make possible the realization of a profit on the investment (including the costs of providing public facilities) simply through the conversion from rural to urban land values. A rational growth pattern affords the means to determine the most sensible placement of educational and other institutions. Less costly

methods for carrying out all urban functions are another result of the predictable, controllable growth that characterizes a new city.

Why, then, have we had almost no new city development? There are four reasons: land ownership patterns; lack of capital; artificial property taxation; and the basic problem of the chicken or the egg—that is, the question of jobs before people, or people before jobs.

Today there is no new-city building industry. Of the thousands of small home builders in the United States, the largest accounts for only 4 per cent of the annual dwelling unit production. We have a legacy of patchwork land ownership; the large singly owned parcels that do exist are seldom in locations suitable for long-term development. Few organizations and institutions have sufficient capital to acquire large tracts of land on the open market and hold them during a necessarily long development period. Property taxation laws often require assessment of undeveloped land based on its zoning capacity or development potential; the taxes thus established are exorbitant enough to make that potential almost impossible to achieve.

As for the chicken-egg question, there are relatively few large new industrial location decisions made each year. Most industrial development occurs in very small increments on three to five acres with employment at about a hundred persons. Secondary employment occurs only through long-term built-up demand for services and facilities—or when two or more of the major department store chains decide to build somewhere ahead of their markets, thereby reaping a substantial reward in increased real estate values.

Housing before jobs, then, seems to be the inevitable order; but purely residential settlements cannot be viable economic units. And there are almost no national, state, or regional development policies regarding location of

industry. Instead, there is dog-eat-dog competition for assessed valuation. To complete the vicious circle, industrial and commercial zoning is not easy to come by unless you're already a live customer. Highway visibility seems as important as rail connections in this rubber-tired world.

On the more positive side of the coin, there is an increasing body of general knowledge applicable to new cities, based primarily on the British and Scandinavian new town experiences. More and more big companies are looking into large-scale land development for diversification or as an opportunity to market their products. Trends toward more creative and liberal zoning controls are widespread, and public attention is growing constantly—the Sunday supplements are full of articles on Columbia, Reston, Valencia, Clear Lake City, and other "new town" ventures.

But "new towns" as we have known them so far are not an answer for America. The population figures cited earlier indicate a clear necessity for more powerful medicine. Therefore, the real question is what will it take to build new cities? Assuming that we have the technical management and know-how, the basic investment funds, and the ability—or ingenuity—to make intelligent decisions with regard to location, access, economic and social balances, what are the major difficulties? In what areas does progress need to be made?

1. *State and regional policies on the location of new towns and cities.* Only a handful of regional planning agencies have been willing to propose peripheral new towns and designate sites for them. At this time, not a single state has indicated locations for new major cities to divert population growth. New York, with its Urban Development Corporation, is the only state with an instrument of sufficient scope to carry out a policy of guided urbanization. But its statewide planning, while extremely advanced, is so general that it does not tell *where* those new public powers should be used. Rather than the federal government attempting to locate such new cities, it should encourage the states to do so; it should use its myriad programs to urge states and regions to develop new-city policies, to guide public and private action. Here the federal role is obviously the crucial one.

2. *Federal leadership and financial aid.* In addition to policy guidelines, financial assistance will be necessary to either provide or insure the large sums of money necessary for land acquistion, development, operating expenses, and community facilities during the early years of a new city. The assistance should be in the form of long-term loans and grants either to public development agencies or responsible private development companies, which would operate within the framework of governmental controls. This "patient" money must be in sufficient amounts to assure the new cities' birth and their growth to a level of self-sufficiency. The financing should prevent the placement of undue burdens on the county in which the city is to be located. Funds must also be made available to assist the county, to expand its capacity to absorb the new city.

166

3. *Programs of subsidized housing, job training, family counseling.* These must be an essential element of the new cities. Priorities must be given to those individuals and families who are willing and able to move from ghettos and can adjust to the differences and freedoms of life in the new city.

4. *The creation of state, regional, and/or local public development agencies to establish and carry out growth policies and generally guide the development of new cities.* Since it would be unreasonable to expect the residents of open country or small towns to have the competence to develop new cities, the development corporations should follow the British new-town corporation model and have freedom from purely local control, in the interest of the larger future population.

5. *Preservation of open space.* An essential component of new-city development will be the purchase and preservation of significant amounts of open country around and in the new city to prevent parasitic development from destroying the integrity of the plan, its systems, and the ways of life envisioned for future residents.

6. *Employment base.* The most important single tool after land acquisition and long-term financing is the creation of an industrial and employment base for the new city. While much of it can be accomplished by proper recruiting and promotion, inexpensive or free land, other incentives will be required. They may include alleviation of federal corporate and state taxes for a number of years, special training of labor forces, favorable rail and truck rates, opportunities for savings through innovative construction methods, and freedom from archaic codes and restrictions. Groups of industries could be organized to work together and build complementary facilities with product linkages and possibly some financial participation in the project.

The most important aspect of building new cities is the opportunity for a fresh start, a chance to put to work what we know of how to build better places to live, to work, to invest, to be educated, and to grow old; places of safety, convenience, excitement, and beauty, places free of all the conditions that make Americans anti-city. The most affluent nation in the world has the capacity to create the most wonderful urban places on earth through public power, public financial leadership, and wise use of private enterprise. All it needs is the political framework within which to act.

REPORT OF THE NATIONAL COMMITTEE ON URBAN GROWTH POLICY

Concern with long-range policies to accommodate impending urban growth is not a diversion from the present crisis in the cities. Rather, it is a necessary step toward finding solutions to this crisis—and assuring that other, similar crises do not arise in the future.

This Committee's concern begins with the needs of the cities and their people. We are convinced that these needs cannot be met without large-scale changes in the present pattern of urban growth. It is a pattern of low-income families living far from the jobs they need; of housing construction for these families lagging because of rising costs and difficulties in finding sites or financing; of increasing division between classes and races in our expanding metropolitan areas. It is also a pattern of the cities bearing a major burden of expenditures while tax-producing wealth moves to the the suburbs.

But our concern extends to the suburbs as well. They are the fastest growing areas of this nation—yet the way they are growing is wasteful and destructive of environmental values. Their residents' taxes increase steadily, yet yield decreasing benefits in terms of the amenities these people came to the suburbs to find. Uncontrolled development is consuming at random the irreplaceable resource of land and steadily polluting the life-giving resources of air and water. Man-made elements of the environment—transportation facilities, water and sewage lines—are being stretched and overburdened by sprawling development. The process is wasteful of money as well: Each extension of these facilities entails a "sprawl tax" of costs that could be reduced by rational planning.

A third group of Americans for whom the Committee is concerned are those who prefer small communities in rural areas but find it difficult to sustain a living there. From their ranks have come, in large numbers, the waves of immigrants to the cities. They came in search of opportunity and have found little but frustration. They should not have to pull up roots: Opportunity should be spread to these small communities so that the painful choice of relocation is not a necessity. If they continue to wither, a significant part of America will be lost.

The Committee believes that the needs of all three groups—the residents of cities, suburbs, and small communities in rural areas—can be met through a national urban growth policy. Such a policy, in outline, would entail the making of rational choices as to the places where growth should occur. It would entail a positive public role in choices of *how* growth should occur so that waste ceases and the end product is a more satisfying environment. It would also entail guarantees that growth will expand, rather than further restrict, the opportunities and options of the poor and minorities.

The instrument of such a policy would be a new center of federal decision-making on the presently fragmented programs that influence growth; a broader state role in the deployment of land and population; incentives to the private sector to locate industries and businesses in places where growth is desired, and to expand its participation in the development process; and new state-chartered agencies to help shape planned development on a large scale. This could take the form of expanding small communities in rural areas, building "new-towns-in-town," and expanding the redevelopment powers of central cities—and creating entirely new communities of city size.

The Committee has concluded that new communities are an essential element of a strategy to shape growth. The members are deeply impressed by their study of new towns in Europe. The European experience demonstrates that new communities can be, from the beginning, places of openness and diversity. They can show just how pleasant an urban environment can be if the full talents of planning and design professionals are brought to bear. They can bring man, buildings, and nature once again into proper balance.

FINDINGS

The Committee finds an inadequate focus in national urban legislation on the problems of growth. Through the years, the Congress has enacted legislation providing federal assistance for planning, housing and urban renewal, construction of public facilities, and other urban systems, but the nation has not yet taken a comprehensive view of these problems. Nor has it recognized the scale of the problems that continued population increase will cause.

The Committee accepts the projection of many demographers that the United States will add at least 100 million new citizens to its population by the end of the century, half again its current population. In accepting this projection, the Committee finds that this many new people will result in severe intensification of the following problems of urban growth:

1. Continued growth of metropolitan areas through uncoordinated sprawl of business, industry and housing on their peripheries.

2. Increasing difficulty of government at all levels to meet the demands of

urban growth and the threat of urban decay.

3. Further decline of central cities without concomitant development of the cultural and other institutional centers which are their hallmarks.

4. Intensification of air, water, noise, and land pollution and further demands on already overcrowded transportation systems.

5. A hardening of the pattern of limitations on housing and employment opportunities in peripheral areas for the poor and minority population.

The Committee concludes from these findings that continuation of current trends will bring the country a succession of one urban crisis after another which will tear at the very fabric of our society. But the Committee feels that the *fact* of growth presents the nation with a positive opportunity to move towards solutions of its problems and the creation of a new kind of order. It finds the following reasons to believe that there is basis for a positive program to meet urban growth:

—The federal government—the Congress as well as the Executive—has recognized the national character of the problems that we face and has created programs in housing, education, job development and other areas. But the money to operate these programs has been inadequate for the task and, with few exceptions, the approaches have been fractionated among agencies and programs. We lack a consistent set of goals and comprehensive approach to the problems. This Committee finds such an approach absolutely essential if we are to find solutions.

—State governments seem now to be emerging from years of inactivity and, through the creation of the departments of community affairs and other innovative institutions, are beginning to devise state-level approaches to solution of urban growth problems.

—The central cities and other local governments, although in a fiscal bind of near-paralytic proportions, have sought and are seeking solutions. But the Committee concludes that they cannot handle these problems by themselves without the financial assistance of federal and state governments and without strengthening their powers of redevelopment.

—There is a rising recognition of the need to deal with urban growth problems on a metropolitan scale, and an outstanding example of this is the emergence of metropolitan councils of local elected officials.

The Committee was also impressed by the growth of interest in large-scale private development in the form of new communities on the part of the private sector. It finds this an encouraging sign and in the best tradition of involvement of business in the building of America. But it also finds that the development of new communities by solely private mechanisms will occur only in those rare circumstances where the dynamics of growth in particular areas will afford a timely and reasonable return on private investment. In most situations, the Committee finds that new kinds of public financing will be required to provide the necessary return on private capital and justify increased involvement of the private sector.

171

The Committee finds that there is relevant European experience in new community building, particularly in Great Britain and in the Scandinavian countries. The order in European metropolitan development and the quality of design in European new communities is worthy of emulation in the United States. But the Committee also recognizes that the United States must also make a conscious effort to fashion its own national policy, suited to its own traditions and institutions, to guide urban growth and encourage the development of new communities. It is towards this objective that the Committee directs its recommendations.

RECOMMENDATIONS

The Committee recommends that there be in the Executive branch a mechanism to serve as a focal point of policy-making on matters dealing with urban growth policy. It should annually report to the nation and to the Congress on the status of urban growth in America, and make recommendations for dealing with urban growth problems. It should be sufficiently staffed and have adequate power to reconcile, among Executive branch agencies, interagency and inter-program differences.

The Committee further recommends that the Executive branch and the Congress, with the assistance of the new mechanism, mold a national policy which coordinates a range of programs designed to assure more rational patterns of urban growth and development in the United States. These programs should include new measures to further assist existing cities to redesign and rebuild, to organize new growth on the peripheries of metropolitan areas, and to strengthen and expand smaller communities in rural areas designated as "accelerated growth centers."

As still another essential component of that program, the Committee recommends that financial assistance be extended from the federal government to enable the creation of 100 new communities averaging 100 thousand population each and 10 new communities of at least 1 million in population. The British experience shows that only new communities approaching this size can be an effective instrument of urban growth policy. This dimension of community building, while it may seem ambitious, will accommodate only 20 percent of the anticipated population growth in the United States by the end of this century. The cost of this program, as seen by the Committee, will be small compared to the cost incurred by the inefficiencies in the current approach to development and the lack of coordination among existing programs. The Committee finds that building of new communities at this scale will produce efficiencies and returns to the national economy which dwarf the direct outlays involved.

The Committee recommends that a national program of this magnitude, established to promote and assist new community development, be predicated on the following principles:

1. New communities developed under this program must significantly con-

tribute to an increase in housing, education, training, and employment in the area in which it is built, with particular attention to the needs of central cities.

2. New communities under this program should result in socially and economically adjusted communities. Special account should be taken of the needs of low and moderate income families. Special opportunities should be provided to afford gainful, varied, and satisfying employment to such families. They should not, however, be induced to migrate to new towns without the assurance of having there employment, adequate housing, recreation, and like facilities.

New towns should be attractive to all classes, creeds, and races; to all types of businesses and industries; to a mix of citizen talent that will insure new town success.

3. New communities developed under this program should be carried out in accordance with the announced planning objectives of the state and local governments of the region in which the development is located. They must be consistent with existing and future national objectives and policy for orderly urban growth and development.

4. New community developments under this program must provide full opportunity for the private sector to be engaged in both long-term financing and construction within the larger planning objectives established by the governments involved.

5. New community developments assisted under this program should not encourage the proliferation of special service districts, and should, to the maximum extent possible, build upon the powers of general purpose state, county, and local governments.

6. New communities developed under this program should encourage the use of the latest technological advances in construction.

7. New communities developed under this program should follow the highest standards of planning and urban design.

The Committee recommends that the Congress enact a program of long-term loans or loan guarantees to assist agencies empowered under state law to assemble land, install public facilities, and plan for large-scale new community development. These loans or loan guarantees should provide for deferment of payment of principal and interest for no more than 15 years, or at such time within 15 years as revenue of the agency allows repayment.

The Committee recommends to states that they authorize the creation of agencies at the state, county, or local level with power to use the federal financing tools mentioned above. The agency—the key development instrument of an urban growth policy—should have authority to operate in at least the following kinds of areas:

1. In existing metropolitan areas, including central cities where sprawling suburban development is the norm, or where inefficient design has seriously retarded growth, and where such agencies can operate as an arm of state or

local governments for the purpose of ordering metropolitan development in accordance with the development objectives of the region. Thus, in these areas, the function of the agency would be to utilize the existing dynamic of growth to bring about a stronger ordering of the forces of growth, thereby making the development more efficient and opening new opportunities to all the people of the region.

2. Outside of metropolitan areas, these agencies would operate as new community builders with the ability to assemble large quantities of land and install the public facilities systems required. These agencies would be empowered to create genuine new communities away from the increasingly congested metropolitan centers of the country thereby bringing about greater balance in the nation's development.

3. In smaller communities designated as "accelerated growth centers" these agencies should be empowered to stimulate growth through the acquisition of large quantities of land, the orderly installation of new public facilities, and the inducement of business and industry to locate in these areas.

Thus, the Committee is recommending federal financing for development corporations, authorized under state law, which could stimulate needed large-scale development in and out of existing metropolitan areas and would have ample authority to bring about genuine balance in urban growth.

Without specifying a specific organizational mechanism to implement this program, the Committee recommends that an appropriate federal agency be established to administer the program and to coordinate with other federal agencies in the administration of their respective programs which relate to and have a bearing upon new community development.

In recognizing the urgency of the problem, the Committee recommends that the federal agency proceed immediately to develop model state enabling legislation under which new community development agencies could be established and operate at the city, county, or state level. These agencies should be public corporations with powers of condemnation and eminent domain, and with an authority to issue bonds and develop other financial instruments as may be required to carry out their purposes.

The Committee recommends that the appropriate federal agency provide a substantial and positive program of technical assistance to state, county, and local governments and to agencies empowered under state law to engage in new community development. The federal agency should also establish a program of research into the latest advances in building technology.

Albert Rains, *Chairman*	Philip Hoff	Henry S. Reuss
James Aldredge	Floyd Hyde *	Raymond Shafer
Thomas Ludlow Ashley	Albert W. Johnson	Robert G. Stephens, Jr.
Hale Boggs	Henry Maier	William B. Widnall
Laurance G. Henderson	John Sparkman	John G. Tower

*Mr. Hyde served on the Committee as Mayor of Fresno, California. He was subsequently appointed Assistant Secretary of the Department of Housing and Urban Development.

174

PHOTO CREDITS

175

INDEX

Exclusion, racial, 32
Executive branch, urban mechanism in, 171

F

Fear, 32
Federal Highway money, 17
Federal Housing Administration,, 32
Federal installations and growth, 119
Federal leadership, new cities, 166
Federal mortgage guarantees, 17
Federal revenues, 31
Flaws, in metropolitan pattern, 18, 31
Foreign immigrants, 41
Forests, destruction of, 81
France, and land deployment, 78
Frederick, Md., 37
"front end" loan guarantees, 114, 119
Ft. Meade, Md., 37
Function of planning process, 75-76

G

Garden city and new towns movement, British, 98
Garden cities (Ebenezer Howard), 104
Garden Cities of Tomorrow, Ebenezer Howard, 114
Gardner, John, 38
General development plan, preparation of, 140
ghetto, 41, 42
ghettos, 32, 164, 166
Glasgow, Gt. Britain, 104, 105
Goals, regional planning, 76
Gottman, Jean, 17, 37
Governmental fragmentation, 136
Granite City, Ill., 98
Grant programs, Federal, 114, 119, 121
Great Britain and land deployment, 78
Greater London Council (Gt. Britain), 105, 109
Greater London Plan, 101
Greenbelt, Md., 94
Greendale, Wisc., 94
Greenhills, Ohio, 94
Gridiron system, 88
Guided urbanization (N.Y. State), 166

H

Hackensack Meadowlands Development Commission (N.J.), 122
Hanford, Wash., 96
Hauser, Phillip M., 33
Hershey, Pa., 98
Hodge, Patricia Leavey, 33
Housing Act of 1968 (U.S.), 114
Housing and Urban Development, Dept. of, 114, 120
Housing choices, 124
Housing patterns, 76, 77
Housing problems, 76
Howard, Ebenezer, 104, 114
Hudson River, 89

I

Immigration, 16
Incentives to individuals and businesses, 112
Income tax, 31
Indianapolis, Ind., 89, 93
Individual alienation, 36
Industrial Development Certificate (Gt. Britain), 102
Industrial development, occurence of, 165
Industrial Selection Scheme (Gt. Britain), 105
Industries, 17
Industry, suburban, 37
Inner city labor surplus neighborhoods, 113
"integration", 42
Internal migration to cities, 31
Interstate highway program, 120
Ipswich, Mass., 87

J

Jamestown, Va., 85-86
Jefferson, Thomas, as planner, 79, 85, 89

K

Kingsport, Tenn., 98
Klutsnick, Phillip, 98
Kohler, Wisc., 98

L

Labor surplus areas, 113
Land acquisition for urban development), 78
Land acquisition for new towns (Gt. Britain), 103
Land, assembly by development agencies, 172-173
Land Commission Act, 1966 (Gt. Britain), 102
Land deployment, public role, 113
Land, loss to urbanization, 18
Land pollution, 37, 171
Land rezoning, 137
Land speculators, 78
Land use, public power over, 78
Land values, urban development district, 140
Land, waste of, 18
Lands Tribunal (Gt. Britain), 103
"Laws of the Indies", planning legislation, 85
L'Enfant, Pierre, 85
Letchworth, Gt. Britain, 104, 114
Levittowns, 18
Lima, Ohio, 32
Loans, federal, long term, 172, 173
Loans to new towns, (Gt. Britain), 104
Local functions, sorting of, 123
Local governments, limitations of, 136
Local jurisdictional boundaries, 123
Local veto power, 46
Logue, Edward J., 114
London, Gt. Britain, 101, 104, 105, 106, 107, 109
Los Alamos, N.M., 96
Los Angeles basin metropolitan area, 33
Los Angeles, Calif., 85
  cult of, 18
Los Angeles metropolitan area, 17, 31

M

Major urbanized areas, 32
Manhattan, 18
Marietta, Ohio, 87
Massachusetts Bay Colony, 86
Medicare, 43
Megalopolis, 17, 37, 123
Megalopolitan regions, influence of city in, 38
Mental illness, 18
Metropolis, 17, 18, 31, 32
Metropolis,
  and federal revenues, 31
  areas, 33
  expanded, 32
  meaning of, 17
Metropolitan areas, 16, 31, 123, 172
Metropolitan council, 123-124
Metropolitan functions, 123
Metropolitan ooze, 78
Metropolitan ugliness, 18
Metropolitan-wide programming, 46
Migration of unemployed, 113
Milwaukee, Wisc., 94
Minorities and poor, 114
Mobile, Ala., 88
Mobility of poverty, 45
Mohawk River, 89
Moravians, 93

N

National Advisory Commission on Civil
  Disorders, 31, 32
National Commission on Urban Problems,
  18, 33, 78
National Committee on Urban Growth
  Policy, 112, 169
National urban growth policy, 170
National urban growth strategy, 115
Natural increase, 16
Natural resources, waste of, 18
"Negro removal", 47
Netherlands and land deployment, 78
New cities, 163-167
  location of, 163
New communities, 113
  and shaping growth, 170
  federal assistance for, 171-173
  rcommendations for, 171-172
New Deal, 19
New Haven, Conn., 86
New Jersey, population density, 35
New Orleans, La., planning of, 88
New systems, flexibility of, 43-44
New Towne Acts, Va. and Md. 1662-1706, 86
New Towns Act, 1946 & 1962 (Gt. Britain),
  102, 104
New Towns, 114, 166
"new-towns-in-town", 170
New York City, 76
New York metropolitan area, 17, 31, 75-76
New York—Northeastern N.J. metropolis area, 33, 76

V

W

Y

Z